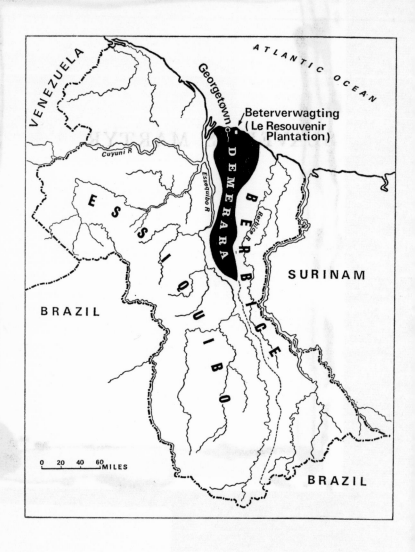

CECIL NORTHCOTT

SLAVERY'S MARTYR

John Smith of Demerara
and
The Emancipation Movement
1817-24

LONDON
EPWORTH PRESS

CONTENTS

JOHN SMITH OF DEMERARA (d. 1824)
JOHN BROWN OF VIRGINIA (d. 1859)

'It was Smith's fate that made the strongest impression, out-side the House of Commons as well as in it. It has been likened in its effect on public sentiment to the fate of John Brown, and it may well have been the decisive factor in starting the last irresistible current of anti-Slavery opinion.'

R. Coupland, *The British Anti-Slavery Movement* (1933)

'In the charge against the late Mr. Smith ... there has been committed more of illegality, more of the violation of justice ... than ever before witnessed in any inquiry that could be called a judicial proceeding ... I have no fault to find with the title of Martyr.'

Henry Brougham (*House of Commons, 1 June 1824*)

'The subject we are now considering is of no small importance inasmuch as it involves a question of the rights and happiness of a British subject, and, still more, the administration of justice in the West India colonies.'

William Wilberforce (*House of Commons, 11 June 1824*)

PREFACE

In the long story of the British emancipation movement the case of 'missionary Smith' occupies a significant place. The episode reached its climax in 1824 when it was recognized as a turning point in creating the surge of public opinion in Britain that eventually abolished slavery in British colonies. The emancipators, notably Wilberforce and Brougham, used the Smith story for powerful parliamentary performances and Macaulay's eloquence on the subject in July 1824 roused a great London audience to high enthusiasm.

The story is here told using the Smith records in London and Georgetown, Guyana, in conjunction for the first time, for which I am grateful to the authorities concerned. I owe many thanks to the Archivist of the London School of Oriental and African Studies, where the archives of the London Missionary Society (now the Council for World Mission) are housed; to the Public Record Office, London, and the National Archives, Georgetown; to Mr R. D. Cheveley for permission to quote from the Cheveley Journal; to the Attorney-General of Guyana, Mr M. Shahabudeen, and Professor Peter Stein and Mr John Hall of Cambridge for help in legal problems connected with Smith's trial; and to the Syndics of the Cambridge University Press for permission to quote from S. G. Checkland's *The Gladstones* (1971). I also wish to thank the Archbishop of the West Indies (the Most Rev. Alan Knight); the Rev. Pat Matthews and Mrs Matthews and Mr Fitz Pollard and members of the Pollard family in Georgetown and New Amsterdam for their personal kindness ad help during my enquiries in Guyana in 1975; and Miss B. L. Morton for making the index.

Cambridge 1976   CECIL NORTHCOTT

7

CHAPTER ONE

The House of Commons Debates John Smith

On the first of June 1824 the tall, elongated figure of Henry Brougham, later Lord Chancellor of England, rose in the House of Commons to initiate a debate 'respecting the trial and condemnation of Missionary Smith of Demerara'.[1]

For Henry Brougham, at forty-six, it was a memorable moment in two respects. He had just emerged from his triumphant defence of George the Fourth's luckless 'Queen' Caroline, and was riding high in popular favour throughout the country. Men cheered him in the streets, innkeepers renamed their inns in his favour, and his one-horse enclosed carriage eventually became so famous that 'the brougham' added its name to the English language.

Whether Caroline was guilty of her offences did not perhaps specially matter to Brougham; his forensic skill had exposed the weakness of the evidence against her, and gave him his little joke, 'the Queen is pure in-no-cence'. Brougham liked to serve unfortunate people persecuted by authority. Caroline was one of them. Could John Smith, who had just perished in Demerara at the hands of the slave owners, be another?

Casting his eye along the crowded benches of the House of Commons Brougham saw the second reason for his rising to propose the motion. It was the diminutive, ageing figure of the member for Hull, his master and mentor, William Wilberforce, aged sixty-five. Twenty years before, almost to a day, Wilberforce had spotted the rising talents of the young Brougham and invited him to join the ranks of the slave-trading abolitionists. Brougham

[1] *Hansard*, 1 June 1824, 1 November 1824.

at once fell under the charm of Wilberforce, and produced a powerful pamphlet, *A Concise Statement of the Question Regarding the Abolition of the Slave Trade* (1804).

Every M.P. was given a copy and so cogent was its controlled invective that the slave trade champions pleaded its undue influence and adroitly urged a postponement of the proposed debate. With Brougham's pamphlet in his hand William Pitt urged on his friend Wilberforce to a division, and at two in the morning on 9 June 1804 the Commons at last gave leave to introduce an abolition bill by 69 votes to 33. It was a triumph for the young pamphleteer as well as Wilberforce.

Such was the man who rose once again in a crowded House and proceeded to speak forty columns of closely printed Hansard on a motion to present a Humble Address to His Majesty.

The Humble Address centred round 'the proceedings which had taken place on the trial of the Reverend John Smith at Demerara' which they contemplated with the most serious alarm as 'the violation of law and justice which had been there committed'. The House was asked to pray that His Majesty 'would be most graciously pleased to give orders for such an impartial and human administration of the law in the Colony as may secure the rights not only of the Negroes but of the planters themselves'. It was an ideal brief for Brougham, the 'old drum-major of the army of liberty'.

A young Englishman of thirty-four had died a miserable death in the jail of a British colony, persecuted by a group of slave plantation owners and managers. He was a missionary dedicated to the cause of goodwill, and was deserving of the title 'martyr'. He had been arrested under martial law, and his so-called trial presented no clear proof of his guilt in instigating the insurrection of the slaves. It was because he had the wrong mental attitude towards slavery that Smith was at odds with the colonial governor and the planter colonists, made worse by his private journal with its criticisms of the treatment slaves received from their owners.

Brougham's masterly handling of this theme not only roused

the House of Commons but so stirred the country that 'Missionary Smith' became a watchword of the abolitionists and infused fresh public fervour for the emancipation cause.

With an astute sense of 'public relations' Brougham spoke to the country as well as the Commons and 'dealt British slavery a blow from which it never recovered'.[2] 'I have no hesitation', said Brougham, in the postponed debate of 11 June 1824, 'in saying that from the beginning of these proceedings to their fatal termination there has been committed more of illegality, more of the violation of justice than in the whole history of modern times, I venture to assert, was ever before witnessed in any inquiry that could be called a judicial proceeding.'[3]

I

Who then was John Smith, the 'calumniated minister', as Brougham called him, whose preaching had, it was asserted, stirred the Demerara slaves to insurrection and threatened to topple the institution of slavery in that British colony?

John Smith was born in the last decade of the eighteenth century, on 27 June 1790, in the ancient market town of Rothwell in Northamptonshire, four miles from Kettering, the home of William Knibb, who exposed slavery in Jamaica, and the preaching post of William Carey, pioneer missionary to India.

Smith's portrait hangs in the vestry of the United Reformed Church, now the successor of the old Independent Chapel of Rothwell whose story goes back to 1655 to the days of the Commonwealth when Independency in the English Midlands was practically the established religion. It is a somewhat feminine picture of a trim young man with wavy hair and sideburns, and a look of fresh surprise about the face. He was not robust as a boy, and it is unlikely that he was given a medical examination

[2] Klingberg, F. J., *The Anti-slavery Movement in England* (1926), p. 220.
[3] *Hansard,* 11 June 1824.

upon his volunteering to go to Demerara. He was already tubercular.

Smith's father, it seems, was a soldier who perished in Egypt during the Napoleonic wars, leaving a widow and family to the mercies of a non-welfare state, and to private charity. Whatever education the boy John received was in the Sunday school of the Independent Chapel where he learned to read the hard way through Bible and catechism instruction.

But what was to be done with him? At fourteen in 1804—the year that Brougham threw in his lot with Wilberforce and the Abolitionists—John Smith was apprenticed to one Blunden, a baker of biscuits in Clerkenwell, London. It was the worst kind of apprenticeship for his health but, no doubt, his mother was glad to see him started in the world. Blunden, the biscuit baker, proved a kindly master and took an interest in the boy's intellectual and spiritual welfare. The Rothwell school taught him to read, but beyond that there was no formal instruction. But he was a reader and read especially at night after the long hours in the bakery: on one occasion his lighted candle set the bed-clothes on fire. He struggled with ill health and fought off smallpox only to carry with him the seeds of tuberculosis.

The Independent Chapels of inner London were Smith's educational as well as spiritual homes. Their pulpits were manned by eloquent Bible expositors who regularly explored the Authorized Version of the Scriptures twice on a Sunday and at least once on a week-day evening. It was a biblical as well as a literary education for a young impressionable man whose thoughts were beginning to turn towards a 'serious view' of his life. What 'the Bible said' became the standard for everyday conduct from which John Smith never varied. He 'sat under' these preachers with envy for they had got the elusive asset of education which he had missed. But in his early twenties it was not too late to emulate them by more listening, more note-taking and more reading. John Smith was on his way to being a minister, and a married one. At Tonbridge Chapel in Somers Town he met Jane Godden (who eventually went with him as his wife to Demerara), and there also in 1810 he 'met the Lord' through a discourse on Isaiah 55 by an eminent London divine, Dr John Leifchild. It 'dispelled my fears', he said, 'eased my conscience and gave me confidence in the mercy of God'. He was soundly converted.

II

It was also a period of rising interest in 'foreign missions' in the London chapels, and studious John had his mind awakened and his imagination quickened by the news of the missionary outreach of the London Missionary Society which was drawing in some £30,000 a year from collections and subscriptions to support its plan to 'preach the glorious Gospel' without reference to denominational loyalties. This ecumenical ideal was the unique badge of the new society, founded in 1795 by a group of Evangelicals—both Anglicans and Dissenters—and its missionary recruitment policy was also unique. It looked not for the learned and the educated to fill its missionary ranks, but for the artisan, the skilled tradesman and the practical man in the useful arts who could take the benefits of civilization as well as Christianity to the heathen.

In its 'Rules for the Examination of Missionaries' (September 1795) the Society said:

It is not necessary that every missionary should be a learned man; but he must possess a competent measure of that kind of knowledge which the object of the mission requires. Godly men who understand mechanic arts may be of signal use in this undertaking as missionaries, especially in the South Sea Islands, Africa and other uncivilised parts of the world.[4]

'Let the hidden jewels be found out, ordained and sent forth', declared the *Evangelical Magazine* in May 1797. A collection of them arrived in the same year at Tahiti in the South Seas on

[4] Lovett, R., *History of the London Missionary Society*, Vol. 1, p. 43.

board the *Duff*—six carpenters, a shopkeeper, a harness maker, two tailors, a gentleman's servant, a gardener, a blacksmith, a cooper, two bricklayers, two shoemakers, a linen draper and a cabinet maker.

There was no biscuit baker among them but this did not deter John Smith from nursing his ambition to go as they did. The *Evangelical Magazine* printed monthly reports of the missions, and these, plus the missionary preaching from the pulpit of Tonbridge Chapel in Somers Town, fed John Smith's hope.

The formation of 'the Missionary Society' was an example of the adventurous action which characterized the Dissenters of the early nineteenth century. Barred from the privileged positions in religion and education, they created their own independent academies and schools which maintained a flow of independent-minded scholars and leaders. Their chapels in London and the growing cities of England were the nurseries of freedom in Church and State, and when their young men turned to go over-seas as 'foreign missionaries' it was only natural that they should carry with them their conception of freedom.

John Smith was one of them and Brougham in his House of Commons speech lauded him with the Independents as:

Men to whose ancestors this country will ever acknowledge a boundless debt of gratitude, as long as freedom is prized among us, for they, with the zeal of martyrs, the purity of the early Christians, the skill and the courage of the most renowned warriors, gloriously suffered, and fought, and conquered for England the free constitution which she now enjoys.

True to the generous principles in church and state which won these immortal triumphs, their descendants still are seen clothed with the same amiable peculiarity of standing forward among all religious denominations, pre-eminent in toleration.[5]

Modest John Smith would not have recognized himself!

[5] *Hansard*, 1 June 1824.

III

With the years of his biscuit bakery apprenticeship coming to an end Smith took the plunge and offered himself to the Missionary Society for service overseas. It was a simple yet astonishing act founded on a belief that Christian truth should be preached to all people in all parts of the world, or, to put it more crudely, that 'millions were perishing without the Gospel'. John Smith did not volunteer to go to Demerara to free the slaves or to work for Emancipation. He was offering to be an emissary of the Gospel and was prepared to go wherever he was sent. It might have been China or Africa.

The officers of the Missionary Society—most of them London ministers and laymen—had simple methods of interviewing and examining possible candidates and in Smith's case the recommendation of his minister was sufficient. But he was still somewhat immature and obviously lacked the poise and confidence that a better education would have given.

The plan for a candidate of this kind was to send him for a period to live in the home of an experienced minister who would guide his reading and be able to give a confidential report as to his suitability for missionary service. It was a blend of paying guest and private tutor. Smith enjoyed his time at Witham in Essex under the eye of the Rev. Samuel Newton who reported favourably on him and regretted his leaving them—it was like 'parting with a son'.

It seems a bit too simple in planning and training looked at with the hindsight of twentieth-century missions and their demand for highly trained experts in specialized fields of service. Smith, like so many thousands of nineteenth-century missionaries, just accepted his commission and departed by the earliest possible boat, and like so many he never came back.

His letter of instructions from the Society signed (9 December 1816) by George Burder, its Secretary, was remarkably complementary to Brougham's Commons speech eight years later when Smith's death stirred both Commons and country:

The Holy Gospel you will preach [wrote Burder] will render the slaves who receive it most diligent, faithful, patient and useful servants; will render severe discipline unnecessary, and make them the most valuable slaves on the estates, and thus you will recommend yourself and your ministry, even to those gentlemen who may have been averse to the religious instruction of Negroes.[6]

Brougham, in his lawyer-like, parliamentary style, put it this way :

My opinion ever has been [he told the House of Commons] that it is alike necessary to the security of our white brethren and just, and even merciful to the negroes to maintain firmly the legal authorities and to avoid, in our relations with the slaves, a wavering uncertain policy calculated to work their own discomfort, and the disquiet of their masters.

It sounds like a modern advocacy of *apartheid*!

Justice to the whites, mercy to the blacks [Brougham went on] commend us to protect the first from the effect of such alarms, and the last from the expectation that, in the hopeless condition in which they are placed, their emancipation can be obtained—meaning thereby their sudden, unprepared emancipation, by violent measures, or with an unjustifiable haste, and without previous instruction.[7]

The House resounded with loud 'Hear, Hears' as Brougham drove home his emancipation philosophy. Emancipation was to be a gradual process and in the eyes of the Emancipators the death of John Smith had been a contribution to the decay of slavery itself. This London biscuit maker, who only six years before had left London to work in Demerara, had revealed the rottenness of a slave society :

The frame of West Indian Society [cried Brougham], that monstrous birth of the accursed slave trade, is so feeble in itself, and, at the same time, surrounded with such perils from without, that barely to support it demands the most temperate judgment, the

[6] Smith Papers (Council for World Mission).
[7] *Hansard*, 1 June 1824.

steadiest and most skilful hand; and, with all our discretion, and firmness, and dexterity, its continued existence seems little less than a miracle.[8]

IV

Brougham was followed immediately by the Under-secretary for the Colonies, Wilmot Horton, a fine example of the urbane, cultivated Tory gentlemen then making up their minds about the abolition of slavery in the British colonies. As a pamphleteer on economic and social questions Horton showed his sympathy towards reform, but there was one aspect of reform that he distrusted and that was 'enthusiasm'. He had made up his mind that John Smith was an 'enthusiast', a person 'impatient to accomplish supernatural results by the intervention of human means'.[9]

This was anathema for the Under-secretary and he proceeded to examine what had happened to Smith in Demerara, through his 'ill-regulated enthusiasm', until he found him 'guilty of actions which, if not in themselves in the highest degree criminal, carried with them all the attributes of criminality to such an extent that they could not be distinguished from criminality'.[10]

As an example of Smith's 'enthusiasm' Horton quoted from his *Journal*, where Smith wrote:

I felt my spirit moved within me, at the prayer meeting, by hearing one of the negroes pray most affectionately that God would overrule the opposition which the planters make to religion, for his own glory... I could not help thinking that the time is not far distant when the Lord will make it manifest, by some signal judgment, that he hath heard the cry of the oppressed.[11]

Horton sensed rebellion. He accused Smith of having preached the 'abolition' of slavery and not 'mitigation' of its conditions—

[8] Ibid.   [9] Ibid.   [10] Ibid.   [11] Ibid.

an 'opinion which is extremely dangerous in a slave colony, and such an opinion is irreconcilable with those principles which the House of Commons and the executive government have pointed out are those means by which amelioration of the condition of the slaves may be gradually effected'.[12] There was, in Horton's view, a measure of criminality in that Smith, he claimed, knew of the plans for the insurrection and 'did not communicate it to the proper authority'. In a lofty peroration Horton declaimed that :

Mr. Smith held in his hands the destinies of this colony, and might have prevented these scenes... I feel satisfied that the House will consider Mr. Smith not as a pattern of prudence, but as a man guilty of the grossest imprudence; though as to the criminality or innocence of his motives, that is a question between his Creator and himself, and, as far as human judgment is concerned, there will be a difference of opinion upon it to the end of the world. For myself I must think him an enthusiast.[13]

To counter the Under-secretary the parliamentary Emancipators put up one of their old and reliable war-horses of abolition, Sir James Mackintosh—Edinburgh philosopher, journalist, lecturer and habitué of Whig country houses. He had been a judge in Bombay and was now member for Knaresborough.

Mackintosh obviously enjoyed the occasion to the extent of forty Hansard columns in which he roamed over the whole field of the Smith case. For him it was a legal, philosophical and emotional turning point in the abolition movement. The 'horrible noise of the whip constantly resounding on the torn and bloody backs of fellow-creatures' could be heard in the House of Commons, 'reminding its members of the miseries of the black host of the king's subjects'.

What if Smith did know of the slaves' intentions to revolt, asked Mackintosh. Men were not 'bound to communicate to the

[12] Ibid.
[13] Ibid.

public authorities every alarm that might seize the minds of any of them'.[14] Obviously (so it appeared to him) the ruling party in Demerara had 'vowed a fierce and furious hatred against Mr Smith'. They were determined to 'get him' and convict him with the instigation of the insurrection. That same ruling party controlled a colony 'where unexampled barbarities were inflicted as mitigated punishments, and held out as acts of mercy'.[15] It was no wonder that the prospect of a thousand lashes and to work for life in irons under the burning sun of Guiana had made some Negroes turn 'king's evidence' against Smith—'such were the dreadful terrors which acted on their minds, and under the mental torture of which every syllable of their testimony was uttered'.[16]

Mackintosh taunted the colonists with their cruel treatment of Smith, a sick man, and, even after his death, at their wrath and eagerness to see his 'skeleton on a gibbet, which, as often as it waved in the winds, should warn every future missionary to fly from such a shore, and not to dare to enter that colony, to preach the doctrines of peace, of justice and of mercy'. As far as he knew, Demerara was the only colony ever publicly to thank a judge for passing so many death sentences at a trial. But Smith, he almost gloated, had escaped them!

Mackintosh was followed, in the adjourned debate of 11 June, by another seasoned contender of the anti-slavery movement, Stephen Lushington—a reformer, staunch churchman, pioneer advocate of the abolition of capital punishment, and then member for Ilchester. Lushington occupied another thirty columns in Hansard, and again rehearsed the case for and against Smith. He had a neat riposte to the Under-secretary's dislike of Smith as an 'enthusiast'. It concerned the divine command to keep the Sabbath holy and to observe the rites of the Christian church. Surely, said Lushington, if this is 'enthusiasm', then a slave state, more than anywhere else, needs it!

[14] Ibid.
[15] Ibid.
[16] Ibid.

V

Then came Mr Wilberforce. No slavery debate was complete
without him and he put his finger on the central point of the
Smith drama. None of the charges against Smith had gone to
the heart of the business, which was that his condemnation was
meant to 'deter other missionaries from attempting the conversion
of the slaves and, by the terrors of his example, to frighten away
those whose Christian zeal might otherwise prompt them to devote
themselves to the service of this long injured body of their
fellow-creatures. We are ourselves upon our trial, and by our
decision men will judge of the leanings of our opinion, where
from the influence of the West Indian proprietors in this country,
and even in this House, we are not in some measure under the
influence of the same prejudices which prevail in all their force
in the colonies of Guiana.'[17]

For Wilberforce the Emancipation movement itself was at
stake in Smith of Demerara. For the first time in the long years
of his crusade he had had given into his hands an example of
the slave system which his own countrymen could quickly
understand and respond to. An Englishman had died in a
colonial jail because he had dared to relate his Christian convictions to slave conditions in a British colony.

This 'unprotected missionary' had been subjected to the
'malice of prejudiced oppressors, bigoted and powerful'. Wilberforce appealed to the House to have 'the disposition and judgment and feelings which justice and humanity and the spirit of
the British constitution ensure from the members of the House
of Commons'. If the constant sound of the lash, and 'habitual
familiarity with the administration of a system of slavery' had
deadened the hearts of the Demerara colonists, it was up to the
House of Commons 'to do justice to the character of a deeply
injured man'.[18]

[17] Ibid., 11 June 1824.
[18] Ibid.

Mr Secretary Canning, then at the Foreign Office, followed Mr Wilberforce with a skilful apologetic speech which on the one hand condemned Smith for not informing the authorities that a slave convulsion was imminent, and on the other failed to define exactly what his crime had been. 'I lament many parts of this trial' (said Canning), 'and most deeply do I deplore his fate; but I do not see, in the proceedings that have been against him, either, that entire exculpation which entitles Mr Smith to the glory of martyrdom, or the proof of *malus animus*, on the part of the judges, which ought to subject them to such a sentence as the resolutions proposed to us imply.'[19]

Canning's next parliamentary manoeuvre was that the House 'take no further cognizance of the question' on which it was 'utterly impossible to come to a completely satisfactory judgement'.

But this was not good enough for Brougham, determined to squeeze out the last drop of anti-slavery evidence from 'Smith of Demerara' and to challenge the speech of Mr Secretary Canning, his rival in parliamentary eloquence. Speaking late at night on 11 June Brougham, in winding up the debate, pleaded that 'the voice of Parliament' should be heard in the West Indies, declaring to the slave owners that while 'the rights of property are sacred, the rules of justice are paramount and inviolable' and 'the dominion of parliament is sovereign alike over white and black'.[20] He accused Canning of ambiguity towards Smith, and of tenderness towards the men in Demerara who had demeaned themselves in their treatment of him. Smith's blood 'cries from the ground' not in vengeance, but for 'justice to his memory and for protection to those who shall tread in his footsteps. . . . If theirs is a holy duty, it is ours to shield them in discharging it, from that injustice which has persecuted the living and blasted the memory of the dead.'[21]

Never was Brougham's rhetorical brilliance heard to greater effect, but it failed to win votes for his motion that 'His Majesty

[19] Ibid.   [20] Ibid.   [21] Ibid.

should adopt measures for securing just and humane administration of law in Demerara to protect instructors of the Negroes as well as the Negroes themselves from oppression'. The Ayes had 146 and the Noes 193, and among the Noes was John Gladstone, father of the future Liberal statesman, grown rich through sugar and slavery.

VI

The parliamentary battle of June 1824 was a major engagement in the long warfare of the anti-slavery movement. Never before had so much popular emotion in the towns and villages of Britain been concentrated upon the story of one man's simple heroism on behalf of a great cause, and rarely had the House of Commons listened to a debate of such a deep human interest and legal importance. Although it was another decade before Emancipation was achieved, the case of 'Smith of Demerara' marked the inevitable end of slavery. Lavish eloquence, and the energies of a group of able men were expended on the enterprise of making Smith memorable, and in bringing the cause of the slaves nearer to triumph.

Thomas Clarkson, historian of the abolition movement, and not given to over-statement, wrote that 'the effects of this great debate cannot be overestimated—this single case of a persecuted individual, falling vitcim to these gross perversions of law and justice which are familiar to the colonial people, produced an impression far more general and more deep than all that had ever been written or declaimed against the system of West Indian slavery.'[22]

The Demerara drama opened on 23 February 1817 (seven years before the House of Commons debate) when the brig *William Neilsen* of Liverpool, with John and Jane Smith on board, dropped anchor in the muddy waters of the Demerara River.

[22] Clarkson, T., *History of the Abolition of the African Slave-trade* (1839).

CHAPTER TWO

Sugar Slave Empire

For John and Jane Smith the first sight of Demerara on a February morning in 1817 was of a wide, flowing river carrying out its brown, muddy waters into the ocean of the Spanish Main. The low lying foreshore along the river was backed by a dark expanse of land reaching for miles inland to higher ridges. This was sugar country and the *William Neilsen* swung at anchor awaiting the loading of the sugar hogsheads for the London, Liverpool and Bristol markets.

Today the modern traveller comes in at the airport twenty miles from Georgetown and drives along the plantation route passing fields of sugar cane and catching the sickly smell of molasses from the sugar factories. Up the Demerara River, bauxite has become a lucrative product, but sugar is still a staple of life for the Co-operative Republic of Guyana as it was in the days of John Smith when Demerara and Berbice were colonies under the direct rule of London. Lying on the vast shoulder flank of South America, alongside possessions of the Dutch and French, Guyana is as big as Britain and as hot and humid as the sugar cane demands. For two hundred years, from 1620, the Dutch ruled Demerara, and only in 1814, three years before Smith landed, did they yield to Britain. Laws and customs were impregnated with the style of the Hollander and the Le Resouvenir plantation, where Smith was later accused of organizing insurrection, belonged to Mrs A. van der Haas, living in absentee affluence in Leyden as the remarried widow of the pious planter Hermanus Hilbertus Post of Utrecht who in 1808 invited missionaries of the London Missionary Society to Demerara to the permanent disgust of his fellow planters.

Today in Demerara 'planter' has given way to 'grower' and 'plantation' to 'estate'. Nostalgic reminders of slavery have vanished but 'Demerara sugar' retains its eminence in Guyana's economy to the tune of eighty-four millions in U.S.A. dollars. For John Smith sugar and slavery dominated the whole of his short life in Demerara.

I

When John Smith landed in Demerara in 1817 the British slave trade had legally been abolished for nine years. But the trade still survived under Portuguese, French and American flags, and even under British ones too, disguised with Spanish names. The discovery on the Thames in 1810 of a ship equipped with 55 dozen padlocks, 93 pairs of handcuffs, 197 iron shackles, 13 hundredweights of iron chains, plus a box of 'religious implements' told its own tale. If this ship had accomplished its aim the profit would have been £60,000 in slave running.[1]

One of the slave-trading tricks still favoured in Demerara was the smuggling of slaves down the coast from the mouth of the Orinoco River. Loaded with slaves from the West Indian islands, the ship would discharge its human cargo at sea into coastal vessels, carrying fifty or sixty slaves, which by night would creep up the creeks along the Demerara shore to supply the Demerara slave market. Sugar demanded cheap labour and the Demerara planter, like all his West Indian colleagues, saw slavery as his source of supply and the returns from sugar ample enough to justify the risks of illegal trading in slaves. Slaves were 'property', as valuable as land and houses, to be 'demised, mortgaged, entailed and subjected to the absolute government of a master'.[2]

It is estimated that in the quarter of a century following the abolition of slave trading Britain spent about £10 million in

[1] Mathieson, W. L., *British Slavery and its Abolition* (1926), p. 21.
[2] Stephen, J., *The Slavery of the British West India Colonies Delineated*, Vol. 1 (1824), p. 435.

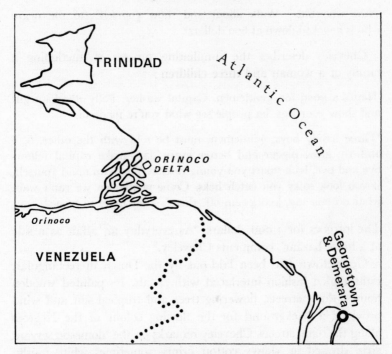

suppressing the trade, mainly on the high seas. Across the Atlantic from the west coast of Africa to the lands of the New World an elusive trickle of slave ships still carried their human cargoes to the sugar plantations, outsailing the watchful British cruisers.

Slave auctions were still established institutions and the one in Demerara was flourishing. A young English merchant, E. C. Cheveley, newly arrived in Georgetown in 1821, four years after John Smith, describes a Demerara slave auction:

Upon a sort of platform stands a man with a black skin, nearly naked, with the exception of a cloth cast about his loin—half a dozen white men are examining his limbs, as you see buyers at home look at a horse. The auctioneer stands by, hammer in hand: 'Capital nigger, gentlemen, name of Joe, good carpenter, aged 28. Oh, you needn't look there, hasn't had the whip often.' Most negroes bear these marks on their loins, many are scored crop and crop with them.

'Now who bids? Walk about and show yourself' (to the negro who is knocked down at 600 dollars).

Cheveley describes the humiliating process of auctioning a family of a woman and three children :

'Here's a good lot, gentlemen. Capital washer, Polly stand up girl and show your legs, let people see what you're made of.'

'Three handy boys, gentlemen, must be sold with the other, 6, 8 and 10, grow bigger and better every day, make capital fellows bye and bye, look smart you young rascals. You Sam mind yourself, if you look sulky you catch licks. Come gentlemen we can't wait, what do you say, knock 'em off, there's a lot more to come.'

The lot goes for 1,000 dollars. 'As everyday an affair as a sale at a horse bazaar', comments Cheveley.[3]

Georgetown had been laid out by the Dutch in rectangular, right-angled fashion interlaced with canals. Its painted wooden houses, dusty streets, flowering trees and tropical sun and wind provided a background for the flowing colour of the Negroes along the main streets. Cheveley remarks on the 'domestic servant girls' dressed in 'showy cotton prints, sometimes white muslin and the head enveloped in the invariable gay striped handker-chief, put on turban fashion, in which these girls well knew how to set themselves off to the best advantage', but he is shocked 'to see many of the negro women, both young and old, with nothing on but a short woollen or coarse check petticoat, tied over the hips, and reaching no further than the knees, whilst the upper part of the body and breasts were left exposed'.[4]

Like Smith, Cheveley called on the Governor of the Demerara Colony, Major-General John Murray. A hardened military man and also a planter with his complement of slaves, Murray could be trusted to regard the plantation owners' interests as para-mount. 'We got to the Governor's house,' wrote Cheveley, 'but he was not within, or did not think it worth while to see us; but

[3] Cheveley, E. C., *Journal*, 1821 (Council for World Mission).
[4] Op. cit.

a youth came into the ante-room into which we were shown and said: "Oh, very well, report yourselves at the office of the Colonial Secretary." This youth, we understood, was the Governor's son, Mr John Murray, and so we came away much edified.'

The same frigid atmosphere met Smith on his introductory visit to the Governor on 25 February 1817:

His Excellency frowned upon me. He asked me what I had come to do, and how I proposed to instruct the negroes. I answered: 'By teaching them to read; by teaching them Dr Watts' catechisms; and by preaching the Gospel in a plain manner.'

Murray could stomach 'preaching in a plain manner', but the naïve suggestion that a Negro might be taught to read was too much for his view of a society based on slavery; it cut right to the heart of slave ownership and threatened the disruption of relations between 'master and slave'.

'If ever you teach a negro to read and I hear of it', Murray warned Smith, 'I will banish you from the colony immediately.'[5]

From then on the two men were in open antagonism.

Smith was not the first of the rebellious race of the London Society's missionaries that Murray had dealt with. Unlike the placid and more biddable clergy of the English and Scottish established churches, the 'London' men were anti-establishment, speaking with the voice of the slave rather than of their masters, and inclined to listen to London advice rather than that of the governor.

Murray knew Smith's colleague, Richard Elliott, as minister of a congregation in Georgetown itself, and there was also John Davies on the west coast. Away in the neigbouring colony of Berbice worked that formidable pioneer John Wray, whose habit of appealing direct to the Colonial Office about the rights of slave assemblies had already caused the recall of one governor.

[5] Smith's *Journal*, 1917. Murray later denied that he said this in a statement to Lord Bathurst (1824).

The handsome Mission Chapel Church stands to his memory today in New Amsterdam.

It was Wray that Smith had come to succeed at the 600-acre plantation of Le Resouvenir, where the pious traditions of H. H. Post, its one-time propiretor, still lingered. Le Resouvenir was soft on slaves. Post used to do all the necessary punishments himself to prevent the cruel excesses of his underlings.

Governor Murray cast a bleak and querulous eye on the fresh-faced young man from London. Was he to be another awkward, argumentative missionary like John Wray? He had no intention of losing his governorship through the backstairs influence of a fledgling missionary, nor was he prepared to weaken on planters' rights and privileges. Slaves at all costs should be kept in their proper place. It took a second application by Smith to get his licence to preach.

With the Governor's warning ringing in his ears Smith arrived at Le Resouvenir, eight miles out of Georgetown on the fertile sugar plain where the plantations ran in parallel swathes with every acre closely tilled with sugar cane.

Lucrative though it could be, sugar planting was an extremely hazardous speculation where 'hurricanes, floods, droughts, conflagrations, insects and epidemics upset the best laid plans'.[6] All the more important was it that the working force of slaves should be kept in healthy and docile condition. Any attempt to ameliorate, improve or modify their lot was a direct threat to the sugar empire.

II

On 9 March 1817 John Smith ascended the pulpit of Le Resouvenir's Bethel Chapel for the first time to preach. The chapel was a long wooden building of green-heart timber from the Demerara forest celebrated for its tough and long-lasting qualities.

[6] Mathieson, op. cit., p. 3.

Alongside the chapel was the minister's manse, a simple but adequate wooden house for his wife and himself. In the morning he had a congregation of 600, and at night over 700 in a full chapel lit with seven candles. The big windows of the chapel were open to the tropical night, and the air buzzed with mosquitoes and flying beetles. It was hot, and Smith, in his best London suit, was hotter still. With his weak lungs he panted through his first sermon, based on a text from the First Epistle of Peter : 'For Christ also has suffered that he might bring us to God.' How much his congregation understood what he was saying Smith was not sure. They were ignorant, poor and doomed to perpetual servitude, Their black skins glowed in the candle light but there was a tired, worn look about their faces and a dull, unresponsive stare.

Smith was pledged not to preach anything subversive that might disturb the planter community or suggest rebellious ideas to the Negro slaves. But how was he to honour this pledge when by reading the New Testament to his congregation he was presenting to them the most powerful of all tracts on liberty for all men? It was this simple but searching dilemma that faced John Smith during all his Demerara years. Week by week he expounded the Scriptures to congregations of slaves whose unremitting labour provided the sugar empire's prosperity. Negroes, whom he dared to refer to as 'brethren', were the despised providers of riches for white plantation-owners who had already sensed the dangers of making slaves Christians without giving them their liberty. Even they realized that Christianity and slavery could not mix. 'What will be the consequences,' asked the *Demerara Royal Gazette*, 'when to that class of men is given the title "beloved brethren"?' To do so, the paper admitted, would make slaves 'as credible as Christian white brethren'.

By his talking, reading and preaching Smith was inevitably opening the road to freedom for slaves, the end of the sugar empire based on slavery, and disaster for himself. Writing of the suspicions of the planters, Smith prophesied 'They would be more solicitous to silence me, than to redress the wrongs of the slaves'.[7] It was a prophetic judgement.

III

In 1822 John Smith sent to London a clear and graphic account of slavery at work on the Demerara plantations as he saw it :[8]

At about six o'clock in the morning, the ringing of a bell, or the sound of a horn, is the signal for them to turn out to work. No sooner is this signal made than the black drivers, loudly smacking their whips, visit the Negro houses to turn out the reluctant inmates, much in the same manner that you would drive out a number of horses from a stable-yard, now and then giving a lash or two to any that are tardy in their movements.

In the middle of the day they are usually allowed about an hour and a half for rest and refreshment : but when they have task-work, not more than half the gang are able to avail themselves of this intermission from labour. Soon after sunset (which is always within about fifteen minutes of six), they leave off work in the field, and each one having cut or picked a bundle of grass for his master's horses, which serves instead of hay, an article not made in the West Indies, they bend their course homewards.

At the season of 'making sugar' night work is added to the day's labour :

Some are employed in grinding the canes, some in boiling the juice, others in carrying away the cane-trash, while another part of the gang is often employed in carting or shipping sugar and rum.

Comparing the sugar slaves with labourers in Britain, Smith says :

The labourer in Britain is impelled to active and persevering

---

[7] *Journal*, 22 March 1819. Bethel Chapel at Beterverwagting is the direct descendant of Smith's chapel.

[8] Smith papers, Council for World Mission Archives.

industry by motive to which the slave is a stranger. The one is stimulated by the expectation of an adequate remuneration, by a jealousy for his reputation, by the fear of losing his employment, by his numerous wants and, in most cases, by the necessitities of a dependent family; and besides, if the work be beyond his strength, he is at liberty to leave it. With the slave, the case is far otherwise. He knows it would be vain to look for reward; and as for reputation, he is quite unconscious of any such thing. If he neglects his work, he is punished; but that is attended with no dishonour amongst slaves : it is too common an occurrence to be accounted disgraceful.

Such labour, against which Smith was a constant protester, was an endless vexation defended by the planters on grounds of humanity. 'Is it not better', they said, 'to make them finish their work on a Sunday, than to be always punishing them.' With no wages paid in money the sugar slave was 'rewarded' in kind—house, food and clothing. Smith wrote :

The huts are usually built of frail materials : thatched with certain leaves, which at a distance resemble straw; and enclosed with wattle, plastered with mud, and sometimes whitewashed outside. . . . The furniture consists of an iron pot for the whole family, and a blanket for each individual to sleep on at night. This is all the proprietor provides for household use. Whatever else the Negroes require they must procure as they can. To make stools, tables, boxes, they mostly steal their master's boards, for which they get many a flogging.

The slavery diet was mainly vegetables and salt fish :

Some of the planters give an allowance of plantains to the slaves every week, but the general plan is to make them fetch from the plantain fields on the Sunday as many as they require, or are allowed, for the week. . . . Where the plantain does not thrive, yams, cassava, Indian corn, and pulse form the chief articles of food. To procure these, the slaves must cultivate, on a Sunday, the ground allotted to them for the purpose. . . . The fish used by them is the salt cod, brought from the British settlement in North America. It is given on the Sunday in allowances at the rate of a pound per week for every working Negro. The children and the superannuated have a smaller quantity. This is the diet of the slaves all the year round, except at the three Christian festivals. They then receive an additional allowance, consisting of a piece of beef or pork, about a pound each person, a little sugar, some leaf tobacco, a couple of pipes, and an abundance of rum, to make them drunk; indeed they have plenty of this every week.

As for clothing. 'the slaves are not overburdened with it by their masters' :

They usually receive an allowance of clothing once in twelve or eighteen months. Then the men receive a coarse woollen jacket, worth about 3s.; a hat, worth about 2s. 6d.; six or seven yards of cotton check; a piece of canvas, to make a pair or two of trousers; a slip of blue cotton, to twist round their middle when they work naked (as indeed they mostly do), and sometimes a razor, and a pocket knife, to pick out of their feet those troublesome insects called chigoes.

The plantation hospital is a 'charnel house' :

Every plantation has a hospital for the reception of the sick; though, in general, a charnel-house would be a more appropriate name. It is difficult to persuade oneself they could ever be intended for the afflicted. Ventilation and cleanliness seem never to be thought of. The excessive heat and the noxious effluvia almost produce suffocation to a person entering. There are no beds in them; the sick lie on a blanket, spread on a sloping kind of platform, elevated about two feet above the floor.

IV

Looking round the sugar empire, Smith came to the conclusion that scarcely one planter in a hundred paid any attention to the moral and social well-being of the slaves. As long as the planting of sugar canes, their hoeing and crushing proceeded with un-impeded routine the local manager was satisfied and, as long as the profits were deposited in their London banks, so were the proprietors. Smith was equally critical of the moral and social condition of the slaves themselves :

The man will simply ask the woman whether she will live with him as a wife, and the woman will often put the question to the man. An answer being given in the affirmative, all is soon settled, and the contract almost immediately consumated; sometimes even before their relations are apprised that such a connexion is formed. They have no ceremonies for these occasions, except those of drinking and dancing, and these, especially the latter, are frequently dispensed with. The honeymoon does not always wane ere one suspects the fidelity of the other; and sometimes the first morning that dawns on the marriage, witnesses also its virtual dissolution.

Of honour or decency they have no sense whatever. They know nothing of the obligations of truth, honesty, sobriety, chastity, etc. They are complete masters of the black art of lying, and make no scruple to resort to it on any occasion when they fancy their interest is concerned. When that is the case, their word is not to be taken, unless corroborated by other evidence.

Slavery itself was the creator of a life which Smith described as of 'the grossest licentiousness' :

The boys and girls work together naked, or nearly so, till after they have arrived at a state of puberty; and herd together like the cattle of the field. After their marriages, if their loose contracts may be so called, it is no uncommon occurrence for the man to go searching at night for his absent wife, or the woman for her husband. As they make no ceremony of entering each other's houses at midnight, the delinquent is commonly caught.

But there was some genuine slave religion :

The patience and constancy of some of the Christian Negroes under severe sufferings on account of their religion, are truly astonishing. Neither the whip, nor the stocks, nor the dark hole, nor their being deprived of their allowance of food, nor the additional work laid on them, can conquer their attachment to their chapel, and the Bible.

The 'diabolical system', as Smith called it, appeared to offer 'no prospect of speedy alleviation', unless by a diminution of the negro population. He prophesied that in a hundred years 'there will scarcely be a vestige of negro slavery in the West Indies'—a prophecy that was reduced in time to a little over a decade by the impact of his own heroic death.

V

The sugar empire itself—although past the zenith of its eighteenth-century affluence—was still waxing in prosperity in Demerara and London. In Demerara, out of a population of 80,000, slaves numbered 74,000, and the value of a healthy, vigorous male slave in Smith's time was about £70, a figure that rose to nearly £100 on the eve of emancipation.

Plantations varied in their slave population from 100 to 600, but the Gladstone family plantation of Success, next door to Smith at Le Resouvenir, had, with its attendant holdings, as many as 1,300. Mr Gladstone, at the beginning of his political career in 1835, analysed his father's (John Gladstone) slave ownership in the strictest 'property' manner, a slave owner's attitude which always depressed and dismayed Smith as he contemplated his mute and pathetic congregations.

The Gladstones at the time of the emancipation compensation owned 63 'head people' worth £87 3s. 0¾d. each; 42 tradesmen at £68 8s. 0½d. each; 12 inferior tradesmen at £38 0s. 0¼d. each; 756 field labourers at £64 8s. 4¾d. each; 250 inferior labourers at £36 0s. 5d. each; 139 children at £19 each; and 47 invalids each worth £11 8s. The total compensation payable was £69,718 13s. 4¼d., an average of £53 5s. 2⅝d. per head. It was characteristic of Mr Gladstone not to decry the farthings.[9] Yet the Gladstone fortune from Demerara was small compared with those of the sugar millionaires of Jamaica, Trinidad and Barbados—the Beckfords, the Warners, the Hibberts, the Longs

---

[9] Cf. Checkland, S. G., *The Gladstones*, pp. 320 ff.

British Guiana Compensation.

Class.	Number.	Rate.	Amount of Comp.ⁿ
1. Head People	63.	£87. 3. 0¾	£5506. 7. 11¾
2. Tradesmen	42.	£63. 8. 0½	£2872. 17. 9.
3. Inf.ʳ Tradesmen	12.	£38. 0. 1¼	£456. 0. 3.
4. Field Labourers	756	£64. 8. 4¾	£48701. 7. 3.
5. Inf.ʳ ditto	250	£36. 0. 5.	£9005. 4. 2.
Children	139	£19. 0. 0.	£2641. 0.0.
Invalids &c	47	£11. 8. 0.	535. 16. 0.
	1309.		£ 69718. 13. 4¼

£53. 5. 2¾
58 - 12
£2. 13

1309) 69718 (53£
  6545
  4268
  392
  £341
   20
  5820
   13
1309) 6833 (51.
  6545
  288

137
288) 8 1
 12
3456
4¼
1309) 3460 (£ nearly
  2618
  862
   4
  3368

Per caput £53. 5. 2⅛ nearly.

William Gladstone's calculations of his father's compensation
from slave holdings in Demerara

and the Codringtons, whose elegant mansions in London and spacious country houses in the English shires were evidence of their prosperity and influence.[10]

Nevertheless when the Gladstone sugar fortune was finally divided among the family in 1851 William Ewart received £150,000, the competence on which rested the whole of his future political career. The Gladstones did not flaunt their sugar wealth in the manner of many West Indian families, yet they could be relied upon to defend the slave-owning interests in Parliament and in public debate.

When the news about the fate of 'missionary Smith', as he called him, startled Britain in 1823, Mr John Gladstone wrote in the *Liverpool Courier* for 20 December 1823:

Whatever evils may be attendant on slavery in the abstract, the

[10] Cf. Williams, E., *Capitalism and Slavery* (1944), ch. 4.

planters are not answerable for them, nor would emancipation be a cure for those evils. The only notion of freedom entertained by the negro is exemption from labour. Place him at present in that state and you ruin both him and his master.

As late as 1833 his famous-to-be son used his budding eloquence, in his early speeches as a member of the House of Commons, to support sugar planters. William Ewart Gladstone scoffed at Fowell Buxton's proposal to pay wages to slaves of a halfpenny an hour. Not only would it add another £3 million a year to the planters' sugar bill, he said, but it would make the slaves lazy, a prospect that terrified the planters and was their prime excuse for using the whip and the stocks.[11]

The sugar dynasties were strong enough to resist the abolitionists in Parliament, but could they thwart John Smith in Demerara?

[11] *Hansard*, 17 May 1833; 29 July 1833.

CHAPTER THREE

Down in the Plantation

In the stillness of the early morning on Monday, 10 August 1818, Smith and his wife were awake in their manse with their ears cocked to a familiar sound. They had been but a year in Demerara and the sound of the cracking whip was already to them the stamp and signature of plantation life.

'Did you count those lashes?' called Mrs Smith.

'Yes. How many do you reckon? I say 141.'

She replied, 'Yes, I counted 140.'

The counting of lashes became a habit of the Smiths as the Negroes were driven past the manse to their morning work on the plantation. Smith writes in his *Journal*:

30 April 1821. I was induced to reckon the lashes and counted 105 stripes on one individual—Philis, for running away.

1 May. Hearing 86 lashes.

2 May. Eighty-one lashes.

3 May. 34 lashes and then 72 more.

The thick, heavy cart-whip—a hideous instrument which tore the flesh of its victims, drawing blood at every stroke—had become the badge of plantation authority used by overseers in the field to punish laziness and by the civil authority to maintain law and order. Smith's sensitive spirit revolted against the misery of the whip.

While I am writing this opposite my window is a poor Negro dancing to the lash of the whip. It is usual to make them lie down when they are punished but this man stands and receives the lashes upon his naked thigh. I counted the 12 lashes. The old man thus punished is attending the manager's cows. Perhaps the reason for this is that the old Negro did not drive the cows up the other road. The way here is frequently not to tell a Negro of his error, but punish him first and then tell him what to do.[1]

Much of Smith's growing detestation of the plantation system and its punishment horrors was due to the fact that he was sometimes the cause of the punishment through his appeal to the slaves to come to his preaching on Sundays. If a manager ordered Sunday work it was a brave slave who disobeyed.

I observed [he writes] one of the deacons pray with unusual affection for such as are persecuted for religion. Last Friday his master had nearly the whole of his men severely flogged because they would not work on the preceding Sunday, and the manner in which he inflicted his punishment added much to its severity. Three stakes were driven into the ground, one for each hand and one for both feet, to which the poor creatures were tied, stretched out full length with their backs upward. A driver was placed on each side of the poor wretches, so fastened, to lash them alternatively, that the job might not take up too much time. In this way they were punished one after another, each receiving about fifty lashes on his naked skin. No wonder so many of the slaves speak ill of religion and say it brings them into trouble.[2]

A year later Smith reflects upon 'the sound of the Gospel of Peace as opposed to that of the whip':

It is delightful to me to see the people coming to chapel on a fine moonlight evening; and from their constant attendance, I am sure it is not less to them. From their prayers I often learn they appreciate the privilege of evening worship. After a deep labour (as field slaves labour) and the harsh sound, and perhaps harsher feel, of the bloody and busy whip, surely the sound of the Gospel of peace, promising rest to the weary, must exhilarate their spirits and comfort their hearts. The chapel was more than half full, and I felt myself at liberty in speaking from Matt. XIX, 27–30.

Behind the whip and the stocks lay the plantation acres of sugar cane stretching in long straight swathes over the flat, rich

---

[1] *Journal,* 17 July 1818.
[2] Ibid., 30 April 1820.

Demerara soil. The glories of Jamaica and Barbados as sugar producing lands had already passed their zenith, but Demerara still produced plentiful crops.

I

It was this fact that encouraged Mr John Gladstone of Liverpool to enlarge in 1815 his investment in Demerara. His shrewd business acumen saw that the Dutch, during their ascendancy, had hardly begun to exploit the fruitful Demerara land, much of which lay below sea level and needed more canals. It was this expertise, and the capital to make it work, that the Gladstone family supplied with such vigour and success that by 1821 the price of a Demerara slave—many of whom had been specially imported from West Africa—was twice as high as one in Jamaica.[3]

The Gladstones' chief property, the plantation Success, became a byword for hard work; here slaves, in John Smith's view, were 'worked to death'. The chief working gang in Success had in 1816 330 men and women organized in military fashion for the planting and the hoeing of the cane. The slave labour force was usually divided, according to age, into three gangs. The 'great gang' ranged between the ages of sixteen and fifty, with women ranking equally with men. This gang was the power-house of the plantation upon which the rest of the machine depended, and its supremacy was acknowledged by the presence of its 'driver' who carried the whip of office flung over his shoulder or round his neck. A woman 'driver' was not unknown in Demerara, and when in charge she was said to be 'peculiarly severe'.[4]

The 'second gang', composed of women over fifty and boys and girls between six and twelve, did the lighter jobs, such as weeding, and this for the children served as an apprenticeship to the gang

---

[3] Cf. Checkland, S. G., *The Gladstones*, p. 125.
[4] Cf. Mathieson, W. L., *British Slavery and its Abolition* (1926), p. 62.

system. Women too old for the fields looked after small children; older men had jobs as night watchmen. A slave plantation demanded life service; there was no retirement from this relentless servitude.

The 'great gang' on a sugar plantation did the work of a plough on an English farm, and this work was considered to be harder than English reaping or mowing. The sugar plant grew so rapidly in the Demerara soil that within a month from planting hoeing was needed, and then came 'trashing' which cut out the dry or dead leaves from the cane, a skilled job which clumsily done could ruin the growing cane.

'Crop'—the harvesting of the cane—followed and was done with heavy machetes, or cutlasses, with one slave gang cutting while another tied the cane in sheaves. The crushing process was a mill, worked by oxen, wind or water power. The liquid was squeezed from the stalks and drained off into the 'copper' boilers for evaporation of the sugar crust. It was a day and night process in the 'crop' season, with long hours in the heat of the boiler house, which made overseers angry and apprehensive about the quantity of the crop and slaves utterly weary of the laborious process which seemed to have no end as season followed season.

In 1824 Mrs Amelia Opie, the Quaker poet, in her *Black Man's Lament*, or *How to Make Sugar*, even made the process look tearfully romantic :

> There is a beauteous plant that grows
>   In Western India's sultry clime,
> What makes, alas! The Black man's woes,
>   And also makes the White men's crime.
>
> But woe to all, both old and young
>   Women or men, or strong or weak,
> Worn out or fresh those gangs among,
>   That dare the toilsome line to break!
>
> As holes must all at once be made,
>   Together we must work or stop;

> Therefore the whip our strength must aid,
> And lash us when we pause or drop.
>
> That mill, our labour, every hour,
>   Must with fresh loads of cane supply,
> And if we faint, the cart-whip's power,
>   Gives force which nature's powers deny.

John Gladstone honestly believed that the slaves on his Demerara properties were treated well, but all his information was second hand. He never went to see for himself but trusted his attorney, Frederick Cort, who supplied him with soothing accounts of the general happiness of Plantation Success. Punishment by the whip, said Cort, was rarely used, and the slaves were able to make money by selling the produce from their gardens. He painted a cosy picture of the Gladstone slaves dressed to go to Mr Smith's chapel at Bethel, with the men 'in nankeen trousers, white jackets and long coats with shoes, the females with muslin frocks, blue silk handkerchiefs and umbrellas'.[5] There, according to Cort, they revelled in the hymns of Isaac Watts and learned his catechism. Many had learned to read, and Cort supplied a list of fifty-one slaves who were taking lessons.

Cort wrote with an eye on Mrs Gladstone who found it hard to reconcile her husband's slave owning with her own and her daughter's evangelical zeal for the Bible Society and the Missionary Society. With one hand they received money from sugar and slaves and with the other supported the causes pledged inevitably to end the iniquitous source of their wealth. It was a dilemma that worried the Gladstone ladies.

Gladstone himself was also uneasy at Cort's facile description of plantation life, and even at the long distance of Liverpool and London feared the signs of possible slave revolt. But even when the revolt did come, and Smith died his pathetic death, Cort, like other attorneys and managers, remained in office, secure in the

[5] Checkland, op. cit., p. 185.

knowledge that they were part of the 'system' built on a slavery that would need more than a revolution to shake.

The flogging of a woman slave, Philis, for 'running away' was an example of the tyranny which so depressed Smith. With no marriage rights, and no independence before the law, the slave woman was in the most pitiable condition of all in the plantation world. Managers had little knowledge of the domestic life of a slave family, huddled together in its thatched hut, with no privacy and little mutual loyalty. Subject to the inherited fears and super-stitions of Africa, plus the whims and cruelties of a plantation manager, a woman had little chance of making a home, even if she knew what that meant. It was no wonder they ran away.

Smith describes in his *Journal* one highly charged 'superstitious' night when the plantation rocked with fear :

1820. Monday, September 18th. For these two Sabbaths past our chapel has been attended by vast numbers of Negroes, multitudes of whom could not gain admission. The reason of this religious commotion is a report that Demerara is to be destroyed by a flood at the next full moon.

The Negroes, frightened at the idea of such a calamity, resolved to attend the worship of God as much as possible, before they were buried in a watery grave.

I suppose this report is founded on the probability that at the approaching equinox the tides will be higher than usual, and if there be a strong northerly wind at the time, it is likely enough to overflow the dams, and do much damage in this low country. I think I never found preaching more fatiguing.

Another was a smallpox scare in 1819 :

Went to the back of the plantation to see the Negroes who have the small-pox. They are in a most wretched hovel. I am not sur-prised at one woman having a locked jaw. I wonder they are not all dead. I could not get into the place. The entrance is not larger than the door of a dog-kennel, not room inside for them to stand up. No light but what comes in at the hole left for a door, and the rain dropping upon them from the roof, and nothing but a litter of leaves for them to lie upon. I never saw dogs put into a worse place.

Slaves.	Proprietors.	By whom sent.
Commerce	Pl. No. 23 (Courantine)	Boullier
Tom	Smith	Pl. Nismis
Joe	Pl. Bachelor's Advent	Pl. Klyne
Fortune	Pl. Bachelor's Advent	Pl. Poderoyen
Thomas	Morrison	Pl. Cuming's Lodge
Welcome	Pl. Felicity	Pl. Goedverwagtig
Dick	Pl. Cane Garden	Pl. Evergreen
Quashy	Stakman	Pl. Industry
William	Spooner	Military at night
Cyrus	Pl. Clonbrook	Pl. Stricken Huevel
Simon	Trotz	S. Thomas
Jonas	Haley	Frankland
Cupida	Pl. Java	Military
Billy	Dr Rose	
Eyles	Pl. Vreedenhoop	
Polidore	Schoon Ord	
Lafleur	Watt	
Quamy	Blundell	By a Bush Expedition, from the Bush on the west side of the River.
Harry	Pl. Vreedenhoop	
Prince	Allfield	
Louis	M'Kay	
Simon	Campbell	
Tronbarry	Schoon Ord	
Phillis	Ditto	
Nancy	Ditto	
Jason	Shaw	Bush Expedition
William	Hicks	Dienders
Hope	Buchanan	Pl. Belle Vue
Louidore	Bennett	Mon Repos
Goodluck	Bentham	C. Benjamin
Martin	Burton	Van Eaten
Christmas	Warren	Military
Tom	Jones	Barnes
Tom	Benjamin	Pl. Vlissengen
Polidore	Pendergrass	Pl. Providence
Amber	Pl. Wales	Dienders
Mary	Long	Dienders
Jacob	Chapman	Pl. Toevlugt
Cornelius / Hurricane	Gravesende	Bush Expedition
Ned	Boskum	Ditto
William	Digh	Pl. Elizabeth Hall
Carey	Pl. Houston	Dienders
Sam	Government	M'Calmont
Kitty	Dr. Rose	Bush Expedition

Slaves lodged in jail and awaiting claimants, from *The Colonist* 11 December 1823, Georgetown

Add to all this, that the doctor has not been to see them at all, this the manager told me and the negroes say the same.[6]

Neglected and in ill health and despised in the human scale of values, the negro had no prospects except that of unremitting labour. A few in every generation managed to reach the ranks of the free through the process of manumission, but that process was controlled by the colonial councils which were all planter dominated.

II

'Missionary Smith' might bemoan the manners and customs of the planter-managers—often themselves 'poor whites' on miserably paid contracts, but an essential element in the plantation way of life—'the men who spend the Sabbath evening over the bottle and the glass, divert themselves with cards and backgammon, are haunted with hideous dreams and fearful forebodings during the hours of their slumber, and then rise to visit their arbitrary malice and authority, it may be upon the innocent slave'.[7] It was the manager who wielded authority over the plantation and set the temper of its life. He could be a humane man, but even so he rarely had a personal concern for the welfare of his slaves. To him they represented so many hogsheads of sugar per year on which he got his commission, and any laxity of control would threaten his job as well as his pocket.

Smith described John Hamilton, the manager of Le Resouvenir, as a 'jack in office' who liked to parade his authority. He came frequently to hear Smith preach and annoyed him by 'shaking his bunch of seals at the end of his watch chain. It appears to be his chief employment during the time of worship; having so many seals he makes a noise resembling the shaking of

---

[6] *Journal*, 29 November 1819.
[7] Ibid., 10 August 1818.

buttons in a bag. I inquired what the noise was. He desisted a little, but still continued clinking in a gentle way. He mostly comes to chapel either to play or to sleep.'[8]

It was Hamilton who claimed that if negroes could afford to buy spelling books they could afford, when sick, to buy their own food in place of the salt cod he provided. It was Hamilton who protested against the suggestion that the flogging of women should be abolished, for without it the slave system would decline in discipline, and it was this remark of Hamilton's that led Smith to record the conviction in his *Journal* that 'the rigors of Negro slavery can never be mitigated. The system must be abolished.'[9] He had come to a conclusion that the anti-slavery forces in Britain had already arrived at. Amelioration and mitigation, while admirable in themselves and, in theory, ardently supported by the plantation interests, were no substitute for abolition.

'Abolition' was a loaded word. It could be used calmly in the objective debating of the House of Commons, but in the Demerara air people's tempers flared at the mention of the word. To preach freedom and liberty from a plantation pulpit was Smith's duty as a Christian preacher, but to link them with Demerara slavery marked him out as a danger to the community. John Hamilton had taken measure of the man at Bethel Chapel. So had Captain Michael M'Turk, a 'burgher Captain' on Plantation Felicity whose job was to rouse the militia for service in emergencies, and also to act as 'medical officer' to the plantations. In 1819 a short outbreak of smallpox gave M'Turk an opportunity of prohibiting church meetings at Bethel Chapel, but this prohibition was in Smith's view so prolonged as to become a threat to his own liberty as a preacher and to the right of assembly for his people. The planters realized that if they could require more Sunday work from their slaves the less chance Smith would have of putting wrong ideas into their heads. 'I have influence

[8] Ibid., 9 February 1821.
[9] 13 July 1823.

over the negro minds, which influence is great,' said Smith to M'Turk, 'and I will use that influence to bring the negroes of the neighbourhood to the chapel, and preach to them in defiance of all the authority you possess.'[10]

III

John Smith was drawing the crowd. Across the plantations on Sunday afternoons and evenings the slaves trooped in ever increasing numbers to Bethel Chapel, except on the Sundays when work on the plantations was enforced.

May 25, 1823: Very few people at the morning Service, perhaps not more than 50. Our usual number is from 200 to 300. I soon learned the cause. The Burgher Captains, M'Turk and Spencer, had ordered the managers in their areas to await upon them with four of their principal Negroes from each estate at 9 o'clock this morning. The planters having been some time in the house with the Burgher Captain (I speak only of M'Turk) the Negroes who had stood outside all the time were called in. The circular was read to them, and they were informed in presence of their managers that none of the slaves must come to chapel at any time without a pass, nor hold any meetings on the estates for religious purposes without permission from their managers. Mr. Spencer, it seems, was very violent with some of the Negroes, particularly with Sandy of Nonpareil. He assured Sandy that if he held any meeting on the estate for teaching the catechism contrary to his manager's will he might expect to be punished. Several planters attended the service at noon. Text Romans 8.28.

Smith became the confidant of negroes in trouble.

Sunday, Nov. 10, 1822 : Jackey of Dochfour and Peter of The Hope came into the house evidently much depressed in mind, to relate, what they conceived an unexampled case of persecution. Their respective managers, under a show of friendly familiarity, accosted the Christian Negroes with taunting jokes on the subject

[10] *Journal*, 2 August 1822.

of religion in presence of the heathen Negroes, representing that their profession was only hypocrisy, and that a trifling consideration would prevail with them to abandon it. Some of the religious Negroes had been provoked to retort upon their tempters in a manner said to be disrespectful—and for this insolence they have been repeatedly flogged and confined to the stocks. The complainants wanted to know what they were to do in such a case. I advised them accordingly.

Smith's advice to negroes in trouble was usually a mixture of pious exhortation to be meek and humble, and a reminder that as Christians they were called to suffer. He struggled with a twin loyalty to his letter of instructions from London not to make slaves dissatisfied and a growing anger at the brutal life of the plantations. When a little light relief broke in to the weekly routine Smith was apt to greet it with a formal primness:

Lord's Day, Nov. 17, 1822: Large congregations as usual. Examination of the candidates for baptism, 13 of whom were accepted. The exposition of the 3 chap. of Ruth gave rise to a long and interesting conversation. I felt it my duty to reprove Romeo for using a very offensive, not to say, blasphemous, expression in prayer, namely that if 'Jesus Christ himself were here, he could not do better' i.e. than I do in teaching the people. It struck me with horror. At noon I preached on John 9.51.

Smith's preaching was a mixture of Biblical exposition and catechizing, leading up to baptism for adults. Baptism became a civilizing mark in plantation life and gave Smith an insight into the living conditions of the people that no manager or owner secured. Candidates for baptism were carefully examined, not only on their basic knowledge of the Christian faith but on their way of life. At one examination an 'old Christian', named Asia, commented shrewdly on the candidates' characters: 'Massa, me tell you know them parents do. Them take no trouble to get their children in the house at night. Themselves eat supper, and if the children no come in if they choose, if not, they may stay out. Almost every night you may find 20 of them sleeping all about, frequently in the horse-stable.' 'Truly discouraging,' comments

Smith, 'and to add to my griefs, a man that I lately baptised and had a good opinion of came with these people in a state of complete intoxication. Surely all the people have not deceived me.'[11]

Bethel Chapel, with its Sunday and week-night preachings, its catechetical groups and baptisms, had become a centre of life for hundreds of workers from the plantations. They tramped to Bethel, not only from Le Resouvenir and its neighbour Success, but from distant Vigilance, Industry, La Bonne Intention, Strathspey, Vryheids Lust, Plaisance, Better Werwagtig, Chateau Margo, Le Beduit, Mon Repos, Friendship, Endraght, Bellefield, Montrose, Batchelors' Adventure, Lowlands—names which echoed the sentiments and inheritances of absentee owners, and gave every negro slave a habitation and home. He belonged to the land he tilled and hoed; the plantation name was his surname as well as his badge of servitude. He was his master's man.

IV

Yet the act of baptism at Bethel Chapel and attendance at services introduced another loyalty which made the slave managers suspicious of Smith's influence. Here was an independent proceeding in the slave's life they could not fully control, although they could hinder its workings. One way was to conjure up jobs to be done on Sundays which would diminish Smith's congregation. He noted its affect on 18 August 1822 :

Though the chapel was well filled I never missed more of the old attendants. The Success Negroes, I was informed, were all at work weeding the Negro yard. Citton was the only one I observed of that whole gang. Quamina was sick. Bristol, our chief man, was sent by his master to catch fish in the sea. None of Van Cooten's people were, and not more than 4 or 5 from Mon Repos, and none from Friendship, nor do I think any from Vigilance, and very few from this estate. Most of them came from a great distance.

[11] *Journal*, 2 August 1822.

Down in the Plantation

The planters' hope of controlling Smith at Bethel Chapel lay in a pass system for Sunday services, which never worked efficiently, many slaves risking 'a few lashes' if caught attending without the consent of their master. But what did work, and amounted to a kind of unofficial partnership between the planters and Smith, was a method of baptism passes. If a slave wanted to be baptized himself, or to have his children baptized, he spoke to his master and asked for a pass that he might carry to 'Parson Smith' as a testimony to his character:

The bearer Parry and his wife Dorah, are well disposed people; so if you think proper, they may be christened, along with their child Pomella. *Plantation Industry, 10th October, 1819. George Donaldson.*

Pass the negro Corry and the woman Philida, to be baptized by the Reverend Mr. Smith. *Plantation La Bonne Intention, 18th June, 1820. F. M. Le Forestier.*

Plantation Industry, 15th April, 1820. I have taken the liberty to write to you, upon the application of the negroes whose names are underneath, belonging to the above plantation, stating their wish to be baptized, and, from my observation of their conduct, I think them real Christians. *R. H. Matthews.*

Names

Loveless	London	Fanny
Colin	Peet	Polly
Prince	Nelson	Codjey
Adolph	Jenny	Fanequa

Plantation Vigilance, June 4th, 1820: The bearers, Cabina, Harry, Juliet, Bella, Chloie, with the man and wife, Berry and Caroline, and their children, Betsy, Patty and Bampfield, have been requesting me to recommend them to you for baptism. I therefore offer them to your consideration. *W. D. Couchman.*
To Rev. J. Smith, La Resouvenir.

Plantation Vigilance, Sunday morning, 25th March, 1821. At foot I beg leave to hand you a list of negroes belonging to this estate, who wait upon you for the purpose of being baptized. *John G. Abbot.*

Judy and child Charles	Nelson
Liffy and children Eliza	Hebe and children, Sylvia,
and Anna	Robson and Magdalene
Pamela and ditto, Sophia	Castor
and Agnes	Bacchus
Juno	Henry
Minerva	Welcome
Aurora	Romeo
Yarico and child Simon	Sarah
Emily	

Parson Smith, Pl. La Resouvenir.

Strathspey, 22nd July 1821. The bearer, Patience, a slave belonging to this estate, being desirous of baptism, and having also informed me that she understands the 'Lord's Prayer and the Creed', I beg leave to recommend her to you as a well-behaved woman. *Will. B. Parrye.*
The Rev. Mr. Smith, Chapel.

Strathspey, 23rd March 1822. Six of the Creoles of this estate, one male and five females, are desirous of receiving the rites of baptism. Wishing to comply with their desires so far as is proper, I beg leave to require of you what it is necessary for them to know previous to their being baptized, and the time when it will be most convenient to yourself. I beg you will excuse this liberty. *Will. B. Parrye.*

These lists[12] produced at Smith's trial in 1824 were regarded as evidence of his widespread influence throughout the Demerara plantations, an influence that was construed to be anti-slavery and anti-planter. As roll calls for secret rebellion, the lists were worthless, but as roll calls of Smith's ministry they were to him

[12] *Documentary Papers produced at Trial of John Smith, a missionary,* pp. 24–5 (Council for World Mission Archives).

signs of what he piously called 'the Lord at work'. He wound up the year with an introspective sigh : 'Lord's Day, Dec. 5, 1822. With great dullness I have dragged through the services of this day. O my God, pardon the wandering and carnal thoughts and quicken me in thy way.'

His *Journal* begins to record other and more ominous signs about his health : 'I find my exertion strangely fatiguing';[13] 'my cough made it difficult for me to get through the service'.[14] But he records with muted glee that on 11 November 1822 a visit from Richard Elliott, his missionary colleague on the west coast, and his wife, had passed off without 'Mrs. E. having quarrelled either with us or her husband'. A year before he summed up Mrs Elliott as having 'a passion like the eruption of a burning mountain; it must have its course and woe to anything that stands in the way of the lava of her tongue. . . . I would not say she is not a converted woman but she is certainly not a sanctified woman.'[15] It was a charitable judgement in the Demerara air where tempers quickly flared. Mrs Elliott later proved her worth in Smith's hour of need.

[13] *Journal*, 16 August 1822.
[14] Ibid., 13 July 1823.
[15] Ibid., 12 November 1821.

RAN AWAY,

THE Negro Man JAMES, the property of the undersigned; well known in Town and on the East Coast of this Colony; he is supposed to have proceeded to Windward, accompanied by a man named Gilbert, belonging to Plantation *Grove*. The usual Reward will be paid for lodging him in the Jail, or delivering him to the Subscriber.

B. S. WARREN

From *The Colonist* 11 December 1823

CHAPTER FOUR

The Demerara Rising—Freedom has come

In the cool of the evening on 25 July 1823 John and Jane Smith
sat in the parlour of their manse at Le Resouvenir waiting for
the congregation to gather. It was a Friday evening and attendance at Friday's preaching, after a long, hard week in the fields,
was always a test of his congregation's loyalty.

A week before on a fine, moonlit evening, the congregation
had been a large one as the moon ensured a safe journey home
along the exposed tracks of the plantations. He had preached to
them on the boldness of the Apostle Paul as he argued for his
faith and worked miracles in the city of Ephesus. Smith liked to
preach from passages of the Scriptures which had ample activity
in them, and this one (Acts 19:8–12) was a splendid example
of the Apostle's triumphant technique.

Smith alternated between Old and New Testaments in his
Bible readings and in text choosing—the more dramatic the
encounter the more it ministered to the cramped routine of his
congregation's life. On 'Lord's Day July 6' he dealt with an Old
Testament masterpiece—Elijah, the cruse of oil, the widow and
her dead son, and was sorry the chapel was not completely full
due to 'Negroes called by the smacking of the whip to attend
other matters during the morning service'. Smith noticed 'one
white' in the congregation.

The fact that he was being listened to and watched by white
planters, as well as the Governor's emissaries, was no deterrent
to Smith. He pursued his simple, unadorned approach to his
ministry, expounding the story of the Exodus and the entry into
the Promised Land with an almost naïve boldness. Every negro
slave and every plantation manager knew what the story meant

for Demerara. But did Smith? Almost unconsciously he built up a catena of evidence that he was actively preaching freedom for slaves and putting ideas of insurrection into their heads.

The plantation air was heavy with rumours that something 'had happened at home'; that in far away London the King and Parliament had spoken about freedom for the slaves. News percolated through the plantation 'bush telegraph' that the Governor's steward had overheard his master talking about plans for freedom, which started a rumour strong enough to reach Le Resouvenir and the Smiths waiting in their wooden manse to begin the evening service.

The messenger of the well organized rumour was Quamina of Plantation Success—a deacon of Bethel Chapel and a respected member of the slave community. Quamina entered the manse with a freedom of entry that Smith had encouraged among his leading church members. Quamina had on occasion been given a portion of the evening meal and a glass of wine. Quamina could read, and was an excellent practitioner in 'extempore prayer' which, in Bethel Chapel, was an outlet for the people's love of devotional speech-making. He was the nearest to friendship that Smith achieved among his slave congregation.

'Was it true,' asked Quamina, that King George 'had sent orders to the Governor to free the slaves?' 'I told him I had not heard', writes Smith. 'If such a report was in circulation it must not be believed because it was false.'

But Quamina was persistent. He was sure 'there was something in agitation'. Had not his son Jack (who used his owner's name 'Gladstone) heard it from the Governor's steward who had heard the Governor 'talk with some gentlemen about it'.

'I told him it was unlikely that orders had been sent to the Governor as the government at home wished to make some regulations for the benefit of the slaves, but not to make them free. This answer scarcely satisfied him.'[1]

---

[1] *Journal*, 25 July 1823.

I

Quamina's rumour was founded on solid fact which, handled by the Governor more wisely, might have avoided the rising and its attendant miseries. The Demerara rising really began in the House of Commons on 15 May, 1823, when Fowell Buxton, with William Wilberforce by his side, rose once again to propose a motion 'that the state of slavery is repugnant to the principles of the British Constitution and of the Christian religion, and that it ought gradually to be abolished'.[2] On the surface it looked like another routine motion of the parliamentary emancipation group, but as Buxton proceeded he charged his speech with an emotional appeal to the Christian conscience of a Britain which had 'one million British subjects in personal slavery'. To avoid insurrection and a 'dreadful convulsion' in the West Indies, Buxton appealed to His Majesty's ministers to transform the world of slavery into a 'happy, contented, enlightened free peasantry'. To the astonishment of Buxton and the emancipators the Foreign Secretary, George Canning, proceeded to put teeth into their resolution. In a wide-ranging speech he agreed with Buxton that 'no Christian will deny that the spirit of the Christian religion is hostile to slavery', but at the same time he held that to believe that Christianity and slavery 'cannot exist together is historically false'.[3] Then came the proposals that surprised the anti-slavery men. Canning proposed that in the British colonies, where slavery was established, the system of 'driving' the work gangs on the plantations by the cart-whip ought not to be allowed; the flogging of females should be abolished; time should be given for slaves to have religious and moral instruction, and the sale of slaves apart from the estates they belonged to should cease.[4] These 'decisive measures of amelioration' were enough to bring Wilberforce to his feet to acknowledge the government's recognition 'that the grievances of which we complain do exist and that a

[2] *Hansard*, Vol. IX, 1823.
[3] Ibid.
[4] Ibid.

remedy ought to be applied'. They were also enough for Charles Ellis, parliamentary champion of the West Indian planters, to plead that none of them was really a champion of slavery and that the whip, it was proposed to abolish, was 'more a badge of authority than an instrument of coercion'.

Within thirteen days a letter from the Colonial Office, Downing Street, dated 28 May 1823 was on its way to the Governor of Demerara, signed by Lord Bathhurst, the Colonial Secretary. The letter summarized the Canning proposals and commended them to the Governor for action through the Demerara Court of Policy. It arrived in Demerara on 7 July, but by 18 August no public announcement had been made concerning the proposals. This was the 'freedom' which had reached the excited ears of Quamina. Smith noted it in his *Journal*—'It is my opinion that the Colonial Government here is acting very imprudently in withholding the necessary information from the slaves, whose minds must, in the nature of things, be greatly agitated'.[5]

II

It was one of Smith's calm understatements of an obvious truth that was further emphasized when his neighbours on Plantation Success, Messrs Cort and Stewart, came to see him to 'enquire what is my opinion as to the state of the negroes' minds in reference to the rumour among them that they are to be free'. Smith tactfully replied that though he did not know the negro mind he was aware of the rumour![6]

By the time Governor Murray had pondered over the Colonial Secretary's directions and hesitated on his action another Colonial Office dispatch on 'amelioration' was on its way from London dated 9 July 1823. By mid-August, therefore, Murray knew the strength of Whitehall's proposals for reforming the lot

[5] *Journal*, 8 August 1823.
[6] Ibid.

of the slaves. The government assumed that the 'driving system' and the flogging of women were disappearing and that Negroes were being freely permitted to attend chapel on Sundays. White-hall had been quick off the mark, and expected even the slow, conservative, Dutch-minded Demerara Court of Policy to do likewise. Murray hesitated, while rumour spread across the plantations that 'freedom' had come but was baulked by the Governor and the planters.

The Court of Policy itself had its first glimpse of the revolutionary proposals on 21 July 1823, and postponed decision until the meeting planned for the 28th which appears not to have been held. On 4 and 6 August the Court listened to Murray's vague remarks as to whether the Canning-Bathurst proposals 'could be introduced and acted on' and wondered whether 'the system therein laid down should not be put in progress here'. No decision was reached, and finally it was agreed that further time and contemplation were needed to devise the best means of carrying out the proposals.

Seven weeks had gone since 'freedom', as Quamina and his son Jack Gladstone interpreted it, 'came in'. It was a vital seven weeks of rumour, mis-representation and ridicule, especially among the Dutch planters who resented the strong hand of the British Colonial Office. Some took away the whip from their drivers in the field but in mocking bravado others served them with two whips, one as a badge of office and the other as an instrument of coercion.[7]

The fears of the planters about a slave rising were not ill-founded, especially when backed by a Colonial Office eagerly issuing 'amelioration' instructions that defied all the instincts of the plantation owners and managers. In numbers the slave population of some 80,000 far out-numbered the white population, and they had access to machetes and knives and knew where rifles were stored. The Demerara Militia could be called out to supplement the small regular army garrison and, as it proved,

[7] Mathieson, W. L., *British Slavery and its Abolition* (1926), p. 128.

the militia, let loose with their firearms, turned what might have been a peaceful revolt into a bloody experience.

The orders from London of 9 July, on the top of those of 28 May, staggered the owners by their comprehensiveness and their promise of a 'further and more effectual reformation'—religious instruction, no Sunday markets, more teaching of negroes, marriages to be established, mothers to be exempted from field work, families not to be split up and sold separately, and no master was to flog until the day after his offence, and then only with three stripes. If he wanted to inflict more than three stripes he had to enter the total in the plantation book and get his entry verified by a magistrate.

So ran the orders from London for the establishment of what almost amounted to a 'welfare state' for slaves. As a planter himself Governor Murray could hardly be expected to be an enthusiastic initiator of these London concocted schemes—this 'amelioration' programme which could only have 'abolition as its final goal'. He could by masterly inaction temporarily avoid London's behests, but he could not use the same tactics with the suspected 'Sectaries' who under his own nose preached liberty from their pulpits and were, he was convinced, at the heart of the rumour and unrest in the Colony, with Bethel Chapel as their base and 'missionary Smith' their leader.

In this spirit of confident generalship His Excellency rode out, with a detachment of Colonial cavalry, from the King's House, Georgetown, in the evening of 18 August 1823, to reconnoitre the field of battle for himself. He made for Le Resouvenir as the suspected headquarters of rumour and revolt, only eight miles out from the quiet of Georgetown. 'I proceeded myself,' he wrote to London, 'having information of a supposed ring-leader at Vreyheids Lust. I turned in there in time to secure him. It was then dark, and a report reached me that Plantation Success was on fire. I pushed on, and at the bridge of Plantation Le Resouvenir passed a body of armed Negroes who disputed the passage, but perceiving that there were not above forty, I returned to ascertain their views.'

In the deepening darkness Murray held his court with the negroes—probably the only time in his governorship that he had confronted such a group. Their demand was 'unconditional emancipation'. Murray says he 'expostulated with this body for at least half an hour and explained how the proposals from London were first steps'. According to Murray's report[8] the negroes replied, 'these things were no comfort to them. God had made them of the same flesh and blood as the whites—they were tired of being slaves; their good King had sent orders that they should be free and would not work any more'.

As they parleyed at the bridge a conch shell was blown and soon a crowd of between two and three hundred negroes were surrounding Murray, who began 'to be apprehensive of my retreat being cut off' and turned his horse homeward to the safety of Georgetown, convinced that Smith and his chapel were at the heart of the mischief. That night he determined to proclaim martial law and arrest Smith.

III

Smith and his wife had on the same day been along the same road to Georgetown and back, all unconscious of the storm gathering round them. They had been to see the doctor in Georgetown about Smith's health. 'Pains and debility' were reducing his energy, while coughing fits made preaching an endurance struggle between his dedication to his calling and his physical capacity. Smith was a sick man and the usual prescription of 'cupping and blistering' his side, while easing the pain and allaying the cough, did nothing to eradicate the decay of his lungs. The Georgetown doctor advised getting away from Demerara to Bermuda or England—hardly the prescription for a man about to lead a revolution!

That same evening the Smiths, setting out for a walk in the

[8] Parliamentary Papers 1824, Vol. 23.

cool of the evening, were handed a message from one of their church members, Jackey Reed, enclosing another from Jack Gladstone of Success, which quite plainly showed Smith that trouble was brewing. The letter from Jack Gladstone was a call to 'Brother Jackey' to rouse the 'brethren of Bethel Chapel' and a warning that 'we shall begin to-morrow night at the Thomas Plantation about seven o'clock'.

Smith was alarmed, for he remembered a chance conversation of the day before between Quamina and Seaton, two church members, after the mid-day service. He heard them whispering about the 'New Law' and 'the Manager' and rebuked them for improper talking. Quamina replied that the 'New Law' had come but the manager had not carried it up to the plantation. Smith warned Quamina of the perils of such talk, and how foolish it was to speak to the managers for they were not the law-makers. Insolent behaviour would only provoke the government, to which Quamina replied : 'Very well, Sir, we will say nothing about it, for we should be very sorry to vex the king and the people at home.'[9] Smith's first impulse on remembering this conversation was to send a verbal message to Jackey Reed warning him of the perilous path he was on, but to prevent misunderstanding he scribbled a note to Jackey begging him to be quiet for 'hasty, violent or concerted measures are quite contrary to the religion we profess'.[10]

The Smiths continued their walk in the gloaming, depressed by the doctor's report on Smith's health and the 'agitation' among the slave population. They met the 'agitation' full blast on their return as they passed the house of Manager Hamilton, where a rowdy crowd of negroes were shouting and demanding firearms. They threatened to put Hamilton in the stocks and, but for Smith's intervention, would have done so. His frail voice was drowned in the noise of the crowd as the negroes finally drifted

[9] Court Martial of John Smith, Oct. 23, 1823 (Council for World Mission Archives).
[10] Ibid.

away in the darkness, threatening the white man for not giving them the freedom which was theirs.

That night the Smiths slept uneasily, knowing that the negroes were in open rebellion along the eastern coast. Smith must also have been aware that Bethel Chapel and himself were regarded as being the centre of disaffection, but the next two days he remained quietly at home, preoccupied about his own future, while the insurgent negroes clashed with government forces across the plantations. During that time he wrote two letters, one to his friend James Mercer, a missionary in Trinidad, and the other to George Burder, Secretary of the Missionary Society in London. To Mercer, who knew the Demerara situation at first hand, he rehearsed the slavery situation, but to Burder he wrote a calm, masterly statement of the cause and development of the insurrection.

It was then that Jane Smith, with a womanly anxiety at lack of news, and concerned at their isolation on the plantation, sent a secret message to Quamina to come to see her, an act which played directly into the hands of the Governor and formed one of the main charges against Smith that he was in association with the rebels. Quamina came between seven and eight o'clock on 20 August—the Smiths' last night at Le Resouvenir—and immediately Smith upbraided him and said how sorry he was 'to find the people have been so wicked and mad as to be guilty of revolting'. Was Quamina implicated? Quamina was silent and, without speaking to his old friends, turned and left the manse.

It was Quamina's last night too at Le Resouvenir for the next day, unarmed, he was shot in the bush while struggling to keep the rebellion within bounds and to make it harmless to the white plantation dwellers. His corpse was dragged to the front of Success Plantation and gibbeted between two cabbage trees, where for months it swung in the wind as a warning to all other would-be rebels.

Smith's two letters—the last he wrote as a free man—rehearse, in a cool and collected manner, the slavery situation as he saw it in Demerara. They were his last testament, the culmination of his six years' opposition to the slavery plantation system and the hideous oppression of the white planter in alliance with the colony government. Even as Smith wrote, Governor Murray struck and surrounded the Le Resouvenir manse with soldiers under orders to arrest Smith on the technical charge that he had not obeyed the 'call up' to serve in the militia.

Smith wrote to Burder:

The whole united colony of Demerara and Essequibo is now under Martial Law. The negroes on this coast, at least, have seized the fire-arms belonging to the several plantations and retired: while in the act of rising they put some of their managers into the stocks, to prevent their escaping to give an alarm; but in other respects, they offered no personal violence to any one; neither did they set fire to a single building, nor rob any house that I have heard of, except of arms and ammunition.

While they were tumultuously assembled on the plantation, and in the act of seizing the guns, I went to see what they were doing, and asked them what they wanted? They held up their cutlasses, and told me to go; I saw that they were infuriated and determined. On repeating my inquiry, they said they first wanted the guns, and then their rights. They soon obtained the guns, and, after giving a shout of triumph, ringing the plantation-bell, and firing the guns into the air, they withdrew. Since then, i.e. Monday evening, between six and seven o'clock, we have neither seen nor heard any thing certain about them.[11]

He then summed up the basic reasons for the outbreak, which left no doubt where his sympathies lay:

Ever since I have been in the Colony, the slaves have been most grievously oppressed. A most immoderate quantity of work has, very generally, been exacted of them, not exempting women far advanced in pregnancy. When sick they have been commonly neglected, ill treated, or half starved. Their punishments have been frequent and severe. Redress they have so seldom been able to obtain, that many of them have long discontinued to seek it, even

[11] Letter dated 21 August 1823. (Council for World Mission Archives).

when they have been notoriously wronged. Although the whip has been used with an unsparing hand, still, it seems the negroes have not been more frequently nor more severely flogged of late than formerly. But the planters do not appear to have considered that the increase of knowledge among the slaves, required that an alteration should be made in the mode of treating them.

However intelligent a negro might be, still he must be ruled by terror instead of reason. The most vexatious system of management has been generally adopted; and their religion has long rendered them obnoxious to most of the planters. On this account many of them have suffered an almost uninterrupted series of contumely and persecution.

The letter was never finished. Lieutenant Nurse with his infantry and Captain M'Turk and Mr Alexander Simpson, full of their militia importance, stood at the door demanding to know why he had not joined the militia to quell the rebellion. Smith's reply was that his 'profession entitled him to legal exemption' from military service. Nurse then played his other, and most important, card, an order to seal up and remove all Smith's papers, including his personal daily *Journal*, and to remove him to Georgetown. A file of men seized Smith, who offered no resistance, and gave Mrs Smith five minutes to pack their bags. She dallied so long upstairs that one of the soldiers shouted to Smith : 'If you don't fetch Mrs Smith, by God, Sir, we will'. Simpson, a planter, enraged at Smith's calm refusal to be a militia man, waved his sword and said to Smith : 'Damn your eyes, Sir, if you give me any of your logic, I'll sabre you in a minute, if you don't know what martial law is, I'll show you.'

The chaise was brought, the horse harnessed, and the Smiths under military guard of a sergeant and twelve men drove down the middle path of the plantation for the last time to Georgetown. There was no friend to bid them farewell, and no colleague to solace their going. Six months of detention and imprisonment and a slow death lay ahead for Smith, as the weight of colony opinion piled up against him as the arch-instigator of the rising.

The Smiths were lodged on parole in a small, stuffy room at

the top of the Colony House for the next seven weeks, while the case against Smith was being prepared. In the hot, airless room, guarded by two soldiers at the doorway, Smith struggled to breathe. He appears not to have been allowed any exercise and was at first denied facility for writing. But on 22 August he wrote a careful, factual account of his arrest addressed to the colony's law officer (the First Fiscal), which again displays Smith's astonishing ability to state a case objectively and without self-pity.

APPENDICES TO CHAPTER FOUR

1. Bathurst's Letter, 1823

In 1823 George Canning, Foreign Secretary, announced the government's plan for 'meliorating the condition of slaves'. Lord Bathurst, Colonial Secretary, then wrote to the Governors of Demerara and Berbice. His letter, if acted upon with energy and resolution, could have prevented the rising of August 1823. This letter also gave rise to the widespread belief in Demerara that 'something good had come from London' for the slaves.

Colonial Office, Downing Street
28th May 1823

Sir,
I take the earliest opportunity of communicating to you the resolutions which were unanimously agreed to by the House of Commons on the 15th instant, and in order that you may better understand not only the general impression of the House in coming to these resolutions, but more particularly the principles which have guided His Majesty's Government in proposing them, and which will continue to guide them in the measures to be adopted for the furtherance of the important objects to which they relate, I have inclosed the best report that I can procure, although it may not be altogether a correct one, of the speech of Mr. Secretary Canning.
'I do not propose in this despatch to call your immediate atten-

Slavery's Martyr

tion to all the subjects to which that speech refers, but to confine myself to one of those points on which I have not found that any difference of opinion exists, and which, being simple in its nature, may be at once adopted, viz. an absolute prohibition to inflict the punishment of flogging, under any circumstances, on female slaves.

'The system of meliorating the condition of slaves, to which His Majesty's Government stands pledged by those resolutions, cannot better commence than by the adoption of a principle which, by making a distinction of treatment between the male and female slaves, cannot fail to raise this unfortunate class generally above their present degraded level, and to restore to the female slaves that sense of shame which is at once the ornament and the protection of their sex, and which their present mode of punishment has tended so unfortunately to weaken if not to obliterate.

I should therefore have communicated to you His Majesty's commands that the punishment of flogging should for the future cease with respect to females, had I not been desirous that the prohibition should proceed from the Court of Policy, as I am unwilling to deprive them of the satisfaction which I am sure they will feel in originating and supporting a measure which has been approved by all classes.

With respect to the practice of driving slaves to their work by the sound of the whip, and to the arbitrary infliction of it by the driver as a stimulus to labor, I am equally disposed to trust to the Court of Policy to originate measures for the cessation of this practice, which I need not to state must be repugnant to the feelings of every individual in this country. I am aware that a necessity may exist for retaining the punishment of flogging with respect to males, though at the same time it should be subjected to defined regulations and restrictions : but as an immediate measure, I cannot too strongly recommend that the whip should no longer be carried into the field, and there displayed by the driver as the emblem of his authority, or employed as the ready instrument of his displeasure.

I have the honour to be, &c.
(Signed) BATHURST

(Parliamentary Papers, 1824)

2. Wilberforce's *Appeal*, 1823

The year 1823 was important in the history of emancipation. In addition to the Demerara Rising it was the year of the foundation of the Anti-Slavery Society, of the first petition to Parliament (organized by Quakers), of Wilberforce's *Appeal to the Inhabitants of the British Empire on behalf of the Negro Slaves of the West Indies* (published in May) and of the government's first steps towards abolition. The following extracts are from Wilberforce's *Appeal*.

The first particular of subsisting legal oppression that I shall notice, and which is at once a decisive proof of the degradation of the Negro race, in the eyes of the whites, and powerful cause of its continuance, is of a deeply rooted character, and often productive of the most cruel effects. In the contemplation of law they are not persons, but mere chattels; and as such are liable to be seized and sold by creditors and by executors, in payment of their owner's debts; and this separately from the estates on which they are settled. By the operation of this system, the most meritorious slave who may have accumulated a little peculium, and may be living with his family in some tolerable comfort, who by long and faithful services may have endeared himself to the proprietor or manager —who, in short, is in circumstances that mitigate greatly the evils of his condition—is liable at once to be torn for ever from his home, his family, and his friends, and to be sent to serve a new master, perhaps in another island, for the rest of his life.

The next evil which I shall specify, for which the extreme degradation of these poor beings, in the eyes of their masters, can alone account, is the driving system. Not being supposed capable of being governed like other human beings, by the hope of reward, or the fear of punishment, they are subjected to the immediate impulse or present terror of the whip, and are driven at their work like brute animals. Lower than this it is scarcely possible for man to be depressed by man. If such treatment does not find him vile and despised, it must infallibly make him so. Let it not, however, be supposed, that the only evil of this truly odious system is its outraging the moral character of the human species, or its farther degrading the slaves in the eyes of all who are in authority over them, and thereby extinguishing that sympathy which would be their best protection. The whip is itself a dreadful instrument of punishment; and the mode of inflicting that punishment shockingly indecent and degrading.

'In my estimate of things, however, and I trust in that of the bulk of my countrymen, though many of the physical evils of our colonial slavery are cruel, and odious, and pernicious, the almost universal destitution of religious and moral instruction among the slaves is the most serious of all the vices of the West Indian system; and had there been no other, this alone would have most powerfully enforced on my conscience the obligation of publicly declaring my decided conviction, that it is the duty of the legislature of this country to interpose for the mitigation and future termination of a state in which the ruin of the moral man, if I may so express myself, has been one of the sad consequences of his bondage.

It cannot be denied, I repeat, that the slaves, more especially the great body of the field Negroes, are practically strangers to the multiplied blessings of the Christian Revelation.

What a consideration is this! A nation, which besides the invaluable benefit of an unequalled degree of true civil liberty, has been favoured with an unprecedented measure of religious light, with its long train of attendant blessings, has been for two centuries detaining in a state of slavery, beyond example rigorous, and in some particulars worse than pagan darkness and depravity, hundreds of thousands of their fellow creatures, originally torn from their native land by fraud and violence. Generation after generation have thus been pining away; and in this same condition of ignorance and degradation they still, for the most part, remain. This I am well aware is an awful charge; but it undeniably is too well founded, and scarcely admits of any exception beyond what has been effected by those excellent, though too commonly traduced and persecuted men, the Christian missionaries. They have done all that it has been possible for them to do; and through the divine blessing they have indeed done much especially in the towns, and among the household slaves, considering the many and great obstacles with which they have had to contend. . . .

To the real nature of the West Indian system, and still more to the extent of its manifold abuses, the bulk of even well-informed men in this country are, I believe, generally strangers. May it not be from our having sinned in ignorance that we have so long been spared? But ignorance of a duty which we have had abundant means of knowing to be such, can by no one be deemed excusable. Let us not presume too far on the forbearance of the Almighty. Favoured in an unequalled degree with Christian light, with civil freedom, and with a greater measure of national blessings than perhaps any other country upon earth ever before enjoyed, what a return it would be for the goodness of the almighty, if we were to continue to keep the descendants of the Africans, whom we have ourselves wrongfully planted in the western hemisphere, in their present state of unexampled darkness and degradation!

While, however, we speak and act towards the colonists personally with fair consideration and becoming candour, let our exertions in the cause of the unfortunate slaves be zealous and unremitting. Let us act with an energy suited to the importance of the interests for which we contend. Justice, humanity, and sound policy prescribe our course, and will animate our efforts. Stimulated by a consciousness of what we owe to the laws of God and the rights and happiness of man, our exertions will be ardent, and our perseverance invincible. Our ultimate success is sure; and ere long we shall rejoice in the consciousness of having delivered our country from the greatest of her crimes, and rescued her character from the deepest stain of dishonour.

CHAPTER FIVE

The Demerara Rising—The Governor's response

With his chief rebel in safe custody Governor Murray turned to
the rebel slaves as they rose in confusion on the plantations.

The militia was his chief weapon—mostly merchants and their
staffs, plantation managers, overseers and some of the elderly
owners who believed themselves 'capable of bearing arms'. Even
the Methodist minister in Georgetown, the Rev. John Mortimer,
rushed to put on the soldier's red coat and do militia duty, but
was politely turned down by the Governor who 'doubted his
efficiency with the musket'.[1]

One of the younger merchant militia men was E. C. Cheveley
who, on the night of 18 August 1823, was roused from his bed
by the sound of a bugle and the news that the Negroes 'were all
in rebellion' :[2]

Up I got, hunted up my military acoutrements, shook myself into
them as quickly as I could. I buckled on my sword, slung my rifle
over my shoulder, found my way into the street, scampered towards
the parade ground, where the bugle was sounding fast and furious,
and the whole town turning out to see what was the matter—found
that the first detachment of the troop had started (we were about
150 altogether) and was soon jogging along with the second detachment on our way to the East Coast—by this time 10 o'clock at
night.

The militia marched on through the night :

Everything perfectly still, save the croakings of all the varieties of
the frog species, which keep up at certain seasons a concert of

---

[1] *Guiana Colonist*, 7 January 1824.
[2] Cheveley, E. C., Ms. *Journal*, Council for World Mission Archives.

every conceivable note, from the shrill whistle of the little lively ditch frog, running down the scale of croakings in alto and tenor, till we come to the deep bass of the huge crapean. These, with the running accompaniment of myriads of crickets, whose continuous chirp mightly fills the air, whilst the thousands of flashing fire flies illumine the air and confuse the eye, were scarcely noticed, so much were we all occupied with what was to come next.

At Bachelor's Adventure they found the old proprietor Lachlan Cumming 'in an awful temper' :

The Negroes had used the old fellow (who was a regular old Turk) rather roughly, and in a scuffle about a musket, which he was endeavouring to load, and which the Negroes wrested from him by main force, he got his nose broken, which presented rather a piteous spectacle. Leaving him in this predicament they proceeded to lay hands on the Manager and overseers, and put them all in the Stocks, to the infinite diversion of the Negro women, whom the Manager had treated with great severity, and who now took it out of him by each saluting him as they passed by him on their way to the interior of the Estate, with a slap on the face, administered probably with no very gentle hand, but by no means an excessive chastisement, considering the free use of the cart whip to which he had inflicted them, and this administration having been completed to the infinite satisfaction of the whole body of the ladies.

One sly old negro, who had often been dosed with salts by his master, 'thought it no bad opportunity to pay him off in his own coin' :

'Here Massa', quoth the old fellow (looking uncommon knowing) 'Here something for do you good'. The manager testified his dissent to this proposal, but the old gent, was not to be done, 'Drink 'um Massa, drink um arl up, 'pose be good for me, be bery good for Massa Buckra, so drink um up 'rectly, I say'. Situated as matters were non-compliance was out of the question so down went the dose. The old Nigger was satisfied with his revenge, and the Manager, who was trembling in anticipation of much worse treatment, not only swallowed the dose, but was obliged to pocket the affront, and the Negroes one and all departed, leaving the hapless whites tied by the leg in the stocks and alone in their glory.

As the morning of 19 August dawned 'the real state of things became apparent', says Cheveley:

We were hemmed in between two large bodies of the insurgents, as far as we could see up and down the road, a dense body of Negroes was moving up on either side, continually reinforced by fresh arrivals, until the road looked perfectly blackened either way. There could not have been less than 3 or 4000, all armed in some way or other, many with muskets, and others with knives fastened on poles. It was an awful moment of suspense, everyone felt that the crisis had arrived when it was decided who should be masters. The plot was thickening, the Negroes shouting defiance advanced towards the buildings, as if about to attack, but halted within about 100 yards, leaving the road clear in front, and thus the two bodies were separated from each other by this span.

Regular troops, under a fiery old Colonel Leahy, had now joined the militia, but a parley with the negroes proved fruitless. When asked what they wanted the negroes replied:

'Massa treat arl we too bad, make we work Sundays, no let we go Chapel, no give time or work in we garden, lick arl we too much. We hear for true great Buckra [the King] give we free, and Massa no let we hab nothing'. To all this the old Colonel would make no reply, unless they would lay down thier arms and go to work.

With his temper rising Leahy once more asked them to lay down arms and go to work. 'No no, we fight for freedom', came the reply. At this Leahy ordered regulars and militia to fire indiscriminately into the crowd, bringing down scores of negroes and scattering the rest. 'Well done, rifles', shouted the Colonel. Cheveley comforted himself that his rifle misfired for 'I repeatedly pulled the trigger without effect'.

The 'defeated and enraged negroes', according to Cheveley, ransacked and fired the buildings of Bachelor's Adventure plantation, shooting the drunken trumpeter of the regulars, and then disappearing into the bush, leaving behind 'a dismal sight of dead bodies strewed out'. He estimates about two hundred Negroes fell in the skirmish.

'We now marched through a burning sun, half dead with fatigue and thirst, having had little or no rest for two nights and days', says Cheveley. At Mahaica they released three plantation men from the stocks 'much to their joy and satisfaction, as they had begun to have queer feelings respecting their future'.

I

Being put in the stocks and jeered at was probably the worst that happened to plantation owners or their managers in the insurrection. Ill organized, with no central director, and no general strategy, except a vague demand for 'freedom', the rebels, as they were called, were remarkably controlled in safeguarding lives and property, and no white man was deliberately murdered. It was tragically otherwise with the Colony's armed forces. Colonel Leahy having, as he claimed, defeated the negroes along the east coast, now conceived it to be his duty to punish the ringleaders. At 'John and Cove' plantation he found the plantation house filled with negroes 'dispirited and alarmed' at his military bravado. Seeing one negro making off into the bush Leahy ordered a corporal and two privates (one of whom was Cheveley) to arrest him.

He was a tall, fine-looking young mulatto man and when overtaken appeared greatly alarmed, trembling all over with agitation. Our Corporal said: 'Come, boy, you must go back with us'. 'Oh, Massa' he said 'you go for kill me—Oh Massa me innocent, we been quite arl de time for true'. 'Well, well', said our Corporal, a good kind of Scotchman, who kept a store in Georgetown, 'well, well, my lad, gin ye be innocent there'l nae homm'. 'Deed Massa me innocent. What for Massa want me, Oh Massa feel in myself they go for kill me. 'peak for me do Massa'. 'Well Alick' I said, for I knew the man's name, 'if you are innocent you'll come to no harm, you tell true that's all'. So we put the poor fellow between us and marched him to the front.

By this time Leahy and his officers had been holding an

impromptu 'court martial' on the principal negro of the estate, and a trusty and favourite servant.

I soon saw from the anxious expression of Hopkinson's (his master's) face, that the man's life was as good as gone. 'Bring that fellow to the front' shouted the old Colonel (looking more awful than ever). There was a dead silence—the Negroes looked on silently and apprehensively. 'Now you rascal what have you to say?'. The man protested his innocence, calling God to witness. The old Colonel roughly gave him the lie, swearing an oath, and reminding him of what had been proved, or rather asserted, in evidence. The truth of this the man denied, and renewed his solemn protest of his innocence. I confess I was much moved with his appeal, which was made in a manly spirit of candour, betraying no sense of guilt or fear. His master, who was a most humane man, and had been an indulgent master to his negroes (as much so as the wretched slave system would admit of) now stepped forward, and said, 'Colonel Leahy I must beg to intercede for this man, I have always found him a most faithful servant, I cannot believe he is guilty, let me entreat you to give his case further consideration'. 'Who are you Mr.' fiercely demanded the old ruffian, 'go back to mind your business, I am sent here to punish these fellows, and by God they shall receive their deserts. Tie that fellow up'. In a moment two soldiers laid hold on poor Dablin—a single coconut tree grew in front of the house—to that they hurried him, forced him on the ground in a sitting posture, passed a rope round him and fastened him back to the trunk of the tree. The poor fellow pleaded his cause and protested his innocence over and over. His master again came forward, and with much emotion said, 'Colonel Leahy, I will stake my life upon that man's innocence, let me beg you Sir not to be so precipitate. I entreat you to spare him till his case can be more fully investigated'. The old Colonel glared round upon him, and said, 'I'll tell you what it is Sir, its of no use your talking to me —you're acting from interested motives, and by God, if you talk to me any longer, I'll put you under arms and send you down to the Governor. If you are afraid of losing your negroes I am not coming up here to be humbugged by you, and have all this trouble or nothing. Let me alone to do my duty, and you may all sleep quiet in your beds for years to come, but if I am to be interfered with, you'll all have your throats cut before you're twelve months older'. 'Pray to God, Daddy', addressing the Negro by the usual familiar term. 'Pray to God'. Then turning to the officer in command, 'Shoot him.' No sooner said than done! 'Advance one file to the front, ready, present, fire.' Two balls in the breast, a minute's struggle, and all was over. The Negroes gave a suppressed moan, some of the women shrieked. The Rifles looked on amazed, it was the first time we had witnessed such a scene. I felt that a soul was sent into eternity. I had been too much bewildered to pray—I reproached myself.

There was little hope for 'poor Alick' who had been a witness of this appalling scene.

'Now what have you to say for yourself?' 'Mr. Buckra Massa, me innocent for true.' 'You lie, you rascal, haven't we the clearest evidence that you were one of the ringleaders'. The poor fellow protested his innocence, whether truly or not I cannot pretend to say. He showed less firmness than the other, and pleaded hard, declaring his innocence of any hand in the rebellion. 'You scoundrel', roared the old Colonel in a fury, 'do you persist in telling me such lies? Do you know you'll be in hell in five minutes—tie him up.'

The poor fellow was thunderstruck, evidently unprepared for such a result. Being in our charge, I and my comrades, with our Scotch Corporal, James Hutton, were the unfortunates to do this melancholy deed. We took him to the fatal tree (from which the body of the other had just been removed and lay close by) and poor Alick loudly protesting his innocence, and entreating for mercy, was obliged to sit down as the other had gone. I passed the rope round him and tied it round the tree, my comrade assisting. I whispered in the poor fellow's ear, earnestly entreating him to look to the mercy of God, through His Son Jesus Christ. It was all I could do—it fell upon his ear; but whether it reached his heart is known only to God. Another crash of the muskets and he was no more.

II

Then began Leahy's and Goodman's march of massacre and round-up through the plantations. Many rebels were shot on the spot but those regarded as 'promoters of insurrection' were tied together by ropes and marched down to Georgetown. One leading negro, Prince of Bachelor's Venture—broke away from the roped prisoners :

'A man gone' was the cry, 'after him men'. Being near the man who had escaped [writes Cheveley] I instinctively obeyed orders, followed by my comrade, and we gave chase. The man, though his arms were confined, made the best use of his legs, and was getting ahead of us, when my comrade, who was a little in the rear called 'Fire, Cheveley'. Up went my rifle, and off it went this time, but as I did not clearly see the man at the end of it, he was none the worse for me. However, my companion took a surer aim, crack, whiz, went the ball, closer to my head than I should have felt to be safe, had I had time to think at all. It hit the mark too surely and the unfortunate Prince fell forward on his face within a few yards of me. Never was the work of death more sudden or more sure. The ball had entered between the shoulders and out at his heart—when we turned him over he was quite dead.

Cheveley was accused among his militia comrades of being 'pro-slave' and of not shooting to kill. Living in fear of the 'terrible old Colonel' and his powers under martial law, many of the militia were 'young unpractised hands turned out to fire at these poor wretches, as one by one they were placed before them' :

It was a fearful sight, some few were killed outright, but many more were struck by the balls in parts that were not immediately vital, and were long dying. As they were shot they were laid in rows on the grass at a little distance, and as we were marching off to the next estate, I saw one poor creature raise his head and chest from the ground, uttering piteous cries. What became of him I know not, as we did not stay to see. Orders were given to cut their heads off and stick them on poles about the plantation, and this the Negroes, their late comrades, were set to do.

74

He describes one gruesome incident he was involved in :

One poor wretch was shot too low, being struck in the bowels, which
protruded in a frightful manner, and he raised himself, crying out,
'I can't dead, O God, I can't dead.' meaning that he could not die.
Two other men were ordered to shoot, after them I stood next, and
I trembled with emotion, unresolved what I should do if ordered
out. These two men fired and still the man lived and yelled out,
till our Lieutenant, Mr. Owen Kerman, in compassion of the poor
creature's sufferings, put his rifle to his head and pulled the trigger.
Horror on horrors it missed fire. Another ran up, and with better
success dispatched him.

For six days the two colonels—Leahy of the Regulars and
Goodman of the Militia—roamed the east coast plantations
with their troopers striking terror into the negro population.
At the cross roads bodies in chains and heads on gibbets were
ghastly evidence of the colonels' ruthless campaign. For months
Quamina's body hung dried and shrivelled and, according to
Cheveley, a 'colony of wasps had actually built a nest in the
cavity of the stomach, and were flying in and out of the jaws
which hung frightfully open'.

It was while the colonels were rampaging through the
plantations that the Rev. Wiltshire Stanton Austin, Vicar of
St George's Church, Georgetown, made a gallant foray of
attempted reconciliation between Negroes and the white planters
—a courageous but forlorn mission. In their fury the Georgetown
whites petitioned for Austin's removal from the Colony but not
before he had come to the conclusion that the charge against
Smith as a 'firebrand of sedition' was false. He had the courage
to speak for Smith at his trial, which eventually cost him his
position as clergyman for the established Church of England in
Georgetown.

With 58 negroes shot out-of-hand (Murray's own figure given
to the Colonial Office in London on 12 July 1824) and some 200
rounded up, for the likely death sentence or severe floggings,
Leahy had done well for the planter community. They rewarded
him with 200 guineas to buy a handsome sword for himself and

a share in 500 guineas worth of plate for his officers. From the West Coast planters came 350 guineas for having saved them from the disaster. This kind of largesse was topped with 1,200 guineas to Governor Murray when he left for home in 1824. For Colonel—later Major-General Goodman, came the dubious honour of being chosen to preside over Smith's court martial—a militia man lording it over the regulars who made up the court! Goodman was also Vendue Master of the Slave Market where a hundred slaves were auctioned between 20 and 28 August 1823, a fact that must have contributed to the slave unrest, although Goodman had been warned by Murray about sensitive opinion in Britain on slave sales.[3]

III

With some 13,000 negroes on the east coast plantations, all potential rebels, the isolated 'big house' of the white planter was an obvious target. The Walrand house at Nabaclis was threatened at 4.30 in the early morning of 19 August, when Mrs Mary Walrand jumped out of bed, opened the windows, and started parleying with the crowd below.[4]

'Look at the lady at the window', the crowd shouted; 'Fire at her'. They did fire and 'struck me in the arm'. Holding up her hands in an attitude of supplication, they again fired and 'wounded me in the hand'. Mr Walrand was dragged to the stocks but not harmed. His negroes remembered him as an 'excellent master' and his wife as a 'very good lady, giving people physic and going to the sick house'. Their servant Billy dragged Mrs Walrand into his room and locked the door just as the rebels rushed up the stairs to ransack the other rooms. There was time in the blood-letting, shouting and abuse to discuss—even ration-

[3] Parliamentary Papers 1824, Vol. 23, and National Archives Guyana Letter Book 20 July 1823. Goodman's memorial plaque in St George's Cathedral records him as 'lamented by the whole community'!
[4] Parliamentary Papers 1824, Vol. 23.

ally—the causes of the insurrection. One of the slaves, Murphy (later executed), said the 'king had sent their freedom, and their owners would not give it'. Mrs Walrand asked where the information came from, and the answer was: 'Parson Smith preached it every Sunday.'

In so far as there was a plan of action it was a very simple one. Bristol of Chateau Margo—one of the most intelligent of the leading rebels—said at his trial:

Our plan was to drive the white people, but we thought they would come and join the soldiers, and come back and turn against us, and we all agreed to put them in the stocks. We were to be very particular not to harm them, but to get the arms to guard ourselves, and the next morning to let them out; we should be that time have arms; and if the troops came, we should then have been able to go against them; we were then to fight.[5]

Firesticks were a favourite weapon. At Good Hope the house was surrounded by Negroes carrying lighted firesticks which they threw into the house and were promptly thrown out by the loyal domestics. At La Bonne Intention they set fire to the sugar cane trash house, while at Triumph fire was lit underneath the house and so gradually smoked out the proprietor.

Some planters, looking to a siege, shut themselves up with their families in their 'big houses' with a variegated arsenal of cutlasses, fowling pieces and muskets. But there was little prospect anywhere of a fight to a finish. Without arms and lacking any generalship the negroes hardly attempted any serious assault on a 'big house' and were content with putting 'massa' in the stocks for a few hours—half fun and half delightful revenge.

It was a non-violent insurrection. Smith's seven years' preaching had sunk into the plantation slave mind one noble truth: 'It is contrary to the religion we profess; we cannot give life and therefore we will not take it.'

Without Smith the insurrection would undoubtedly have been a bloody one. He may have been tardy in informing the govern-

[5] Parliamentary Papers 1824, Vol. 23.

ment of the bold and boastful talk that was going on across the plantations about freedom. Perhaps he did not take his negro congregation seriously enough nor value sufficiently the impact of his preaching and teaching. He was a modest expositor, and in his almost simple naïveté did not realize the effect of it all on those little plantation groups huddled together after a long day's labour in the fields.

The most revolutionary text his accusers flung at him was Luke 19:41, where Christ wept over Jerusalem and prophesied its destruction, and the most momentous demand he made was for both masters and slaves to keep the Sabbath day as a non-working day in order to worship Almighty God. If this was the stuff of revolution then Smith was a revolutionary, and Governor Murray was correct in assuming that the 'mischief was plotted at Bethel Chapel'.

But it was the Georgetown clergyman, S. W. Austin, who having gone to see for himself and having changed his mind about Smith saw him as the saviour of this 'ill-fated country' and the instrument which 'prevented a dreadful effusion of blood here'. As he watched the preparations of the authorities to arraign Smith he concluded 'that they were seeking the life of the man whose teaching had saved theirs'.[6]

[6] Wallbridge, E. A., *Martyr of Demerara* (1848).

CHAPTER SIX

The Court Martial of John Smith

A British Crown Colony Governor in the early nineteenth century was his own law. He was 'His Excellency' in all things and his elected council usually his ready and willing servant.

John Murray, sometime Colonel of the 96th Foot, with a regular soldier's outlook, was no exception to the colonial pattern, and neither was his 'Court of Policy', the supreme Demerara Court. Composed mainly of colonists, plantation owners and their managers and acolytes of varying kinds, it was officially the instrument of government directly under the Colonial Office. But it was also sensitive to the Governor's temper and responsive to his handling

By his proclamation of martial law on 18 August 1823, and maintenance of it for five months, Murray created a working dictatorship which suited his style of governorship. It was a phoney and fictitious invention which gave him power to meet what he genuinely believed was a colony-wide rising, and above all to bring 'missionary Smith' to trial and sentence.

His prisoner was now lodged with his wife, according to Murray's own later description to Lord Bathurst, in a 'commodious bedroom' in Colony House usually reserved for members of the Court of Policy. They had the freedom of the house and ran up a bill for food, luxuries and entertainment of friends amounting to £300.[1] Murray claimed that Smith had lodgings far superior to his own, and that he was only later more closely confined because he broke his parole by going out of the house to get air and exercise. A sentinel was then posted at his

[1] Murray to Bathurst, Colonial Office Papers, 10 July 1824, written in London after Murray's recall.

door in order to ensure obedience to the Governor's orders.

Stories of Smith's last wretched incarceration in a damp dungeon of Georgetown jail were made much of by the anti-slavery propagandists in Britain. Was it true, Murray was asked by Bathurst, that Smith, after his death sentence, was 'removed to a low damp room in the jail'. Murray's defence was to throw the onus of decision on to Smith himself who, he said, complained that the damp air passing 'through the seams of the floor was unpleasant'. To meet Smith's wishes, said Murray, 'every seam was caulked with oakum and made perfectly tight'.[2]

Writing in Demerara itself, twenty years after the insurrection, and with local evidence still available, E. A. Wallbridge describes Smith's unwholesome cell as a 'room on the ground floor with stagnant water beneath, whose pernicious miasma, passing through the joints of the floor, some of the boards of which were a quarter of an inch apart, were of deadly influence to him in his weak condition'.[3]

Smith was a very sick man whose faint and only hope of living in Demerara was the country air of Le Resouvenir. Three months of the close humidity of Georgetown, whether in Colony House or Colony Jail, sealed his end and, destroyed all his chances in the long fight against tuberculosis. Murray, though medically warned of Smith's condition, was only eager to set up his court martial and gave no attention to the physical welfare of his prisoner. He disputed the charge that he 'imprisoned the Smiths without clean linen' and claimed that Mrs Smith herself was never imprisoned 'either with or without clean linen'.[4]

Henry Brougham in the House of Commons[6] castigated Murray's conception of martial law as 'entirely unkown to the law of England', and therefore an illegal court in Demerara. He recognized the authority of a Mutiny Act and the trial of mili-

2 Ibid.
3 Wallbridge, E. A., *Martyr of Demerara*, p. 133.
4 Murray to Bathurst, 10 July 1824.
5 *Hansard*, 1 June 1824.

tary persons before military tribunals, but to bring a civilian before a military tribunal, such as the Demerara court, was contrary to English legal practice. Brougham also brushed aside Murray's claim that the court martial was an advantage to Smith as the members would be less prejudiced than a civil court drawn from local people.[6] A civil trial would have given Smith the great advantage of having a presiding judge who knew the law and had had experience of sifting evidence and deciding between hearsay and the truth. 'He would have stood forth single and supreme', said Brougham, 'as the judge who tried the prisoner. In such circumstances he must have conducted himself with an entire regard to his professional character, to his responsibility as a judge, and to his credit as a lawyer.'[7]

Ironically enough, the only man capable of being such a judge was Charles Wray, then Chief Justice of the Colony of Demerara and Essequibo. But under pressure from the Governor, in order to lend some legal respectability to the court martial, Wray had agreed, in Brougham's phrase, 'to cover his forensic robe under martial armour'. He appears as Lieutenant-Colonel Charles Wray, Militia Staff, and number one member of the General Court Martial. Wray was the only lawyer in the court, and was compelled to sit 'helpless and unresisting, and see others abandoning principles and forms which he durst not have abandoned had he been sitting above in his own court, in his ermine robe, administering the civil law'.[8]

But the scandal of the Court's composition was deepened by Murray's choice of its President in Lieutenant-Colonel Stephen Arthur Goodman, a half-pay regular soldier of the 48th Regiment who commanded the Georgetown Militia and also held the lucrative public office of Vendue Master in the Colony. It was his business to sell slaves when they came under the authority of the courts of justice and to draw his commission accordingly. Holding up a copy of the *Colonial Gazette* to the astonished House of Commons, Brougham pointed to the advertised sale of some eighty slaves—'valuable carpenters, boat

[6] Ibid.　　　[7] Ibid.　　　[8] Ibid.

81

builders, prime single men, a woman and three children, a female slave who is pregnant'—on the very eve of the slave rising and under the signature of 'S. A. Goodman'. With polite sarcasm Brougham supposed that none of this was 'likely to warp his judgment' but contended that Goodman 'was one of the last men to select as the President of the Court'.[9] The rest of the Court's fifteen members were regular officers from the Georgetown garrison, eight from the Royal North British Fusiliers and the others artillerymen and engineers. The prosecution was in the hands of the Judge Advocate with three assistants.

I

Such was the formidable court that Murray had assembled to deal with 'missionary Smith' and all that Smith represented in the Colony. He had taken three months to nominate its members and to prepare the charges against Smith, and appeared to have an unanswerable case for the prisoner to face.

During those three months Smith was confined to his room with little opportunity to prepare his defence, while in the Georgetown barracks the executions and floggings of slaves convicted of rebellion proceeded at their deadly pace, spreading gloom over the town. A monotonous procession of accused slaves moved in and out of the dock, some pleading for mercy and others resigned to their fate. Their evidence too was monotonous, as if the prosecution put the required words into their mouths.

The charge against the slave Kinsale, of Bachelor's Adventure, is typical of the Court's procedure :

John Munro, being duly sworn, deposed as follows : viz : I am an overseer on Enterprize and Bachelors Adventure; I live on the former; the prisoner 'Kinsale' ordered me to put my two feet in stocks; I said I would only put one; a stranger then said, if I

9 Ibid.

would not put two he would chop my head off; I then put my two feet in the stocks, and the prisoner locked them; this is the same time Mr. Bowerbank who was with me speaks of.

Francois, a negro belonging to Plantation Bee Hive, says he understands the nature of an oath; and being then duly sworn, deposed as follows : I am a field negro on Plantation Bee Hive; I know the prisoner, his name is Kinsale; I did not know him before the beginning of the rebellion; about the middle of the day the prisoner Kinsale came to the Bee Hive, he was with about twenty others; he inquired where Francois (meaning me) was; the prisoner had a musket; I replied I am here; he said, you want to help the white people do you? he said, they must kill me; another one said, you must not kill him, but carry him with us and make him fight; they carried me with them, and Kinsale gave me a fowling piece; he had a musket himself at the same time; he then went to Rogers's Koker, where there was a collection of people, where Kinsale told January that I was the man killed the black man Andrew (who had been shot by the soldiers), and they wanted to kill me for it; they went away, tied me, and a man named Ned of Clonbrook took me to the stocks and put me in, both feet; Ned took away the fowling-piece.

The prisoner being asked what he had to say in his defence, stated; I am very sorry at having committed what I have done; I beg the Court's pardon for it and I am sure I shall never do the like again.

The Court having most maturely and deliberately weighed and considered the evidence adduced in support of the Charge preferred against the prisoner Kinsale, as well as the statement made by him in his defence, is of opinion that he the prisoner Kinsale is guilty of the charge preferred against him, and does therefore sentence him, the prisoner Kinsale, to be hanged by the neck until he be dead, at such time and place as His Excellency the Commander-in-Chief may deem fit.

V. A. Heyliger, Judge Advocate,   S. A. Goodman,
(Approved) Jno. Murray,   Lieut-Col. etc., President.
Comm-in-Chief.

Kinsale was one of the fifteen condemned men recommended to

'receive the King's pardon and to be banished to Bermuda';.[10] the most notable was Jack Gladstone of Success.

The possibility of pardon was a dazzling prize for the convicted negroes, particularly when it could easily be got by providing evidence against Smith. This was Murray's secret weapon in the weeks before Smith was brought into the dock. His lawyers were busy in the colony jail taking evidence, writing stories, and concocting information all beamed on denigrating Smith and fastening the cause of the insurrection on to him.

Jack Gladstone of Success was Murray's favourite prisoner, an 'athletic young man', he told Lord Bathurst, 'and of that open and manly disposition which would naturally lead him to enter with heart and hand upon his undertakings... who heartily co-operated with his father Quamina in maturing and carrying into effect a plot he had been given to hope must procure for both a release from bondage'.[11]

With the perjured evidence of Jack and two others, Paris and Sandy, in his hand Murray felt confident about the conviction of Smith. To have executed Jack at once in response to public clamour would have weakened his evidence against Smith. Had not Jack prophesied that in the new all black empire of Demerara Smith would be emperor, his father king and himself prince?[12] Jack was taunted by the *Demerara Gazette* with wallowing in the 'comforting consciousness of his own reprieve', while his former friends and conspiritors 'suffered the full penalty of the lash'. No doubt Jack Gladstone had a full view of the sufferings he had assisted to bring, upon his fellow slaves—'Louis of Porter's Hope, 1,000 lashes, Field of Clonbrook, 1,000, Mercury of Enmore, 700, Austin of Cove, 1,000, Tessamin of Success, 1,000, John Otto, 200, August of 'Success, 600':.'[13]

[10] Parliamentary Papers 1824, Vol. 23.
[11] Ibid.   [12] Ibid.
[13] *Demerara Gazette*, 16 January 1824. According to an inventory (C.O. 1824:58), the total number of lashes inflicted as a result of the insurrection was 12,500.

Murray argued that his reprieve of Jack was entirely political and part of his policy of showing the slaves that when they safeguarded the lives and property of white people, as Jack undoubtedly had done, their acts should not 'be lost sight of in awarding a punishment for their crimes'.[14] But the target always was Smith.

All during September 1823 Murray and his lawyers were fashioning the charges against Smith and eventually shaped them into four main accusations :

1 That he did promote discontent and dissatisfaction in the minds of negro slaves towards their lawful masters, managers and overseers, thereby intending to incite the said negroes to break out into open revolt and against the peace of our Sovereign Lord the King.
2 Having advised, consulted and corresponded with a certain negro named Quamina touching an intended revolt, and did aid and assist such a rebellion.
3 Having come to the knowledge of a certain revolt and rebellion he did not make known the same to the proper authorities.
4 Well knowing the said Quamina to be an insurgent he did not use his utmost endeavours to secure and detain the said Quamina as a prisoner but permitted him to go at large and depart against the peace of our Sovereign Lord the King.

Brougham described the charges as 'artfully drawn up', so that the prisoner was never aware of the 'specific accusation against him'. As well as 'artful' they were 'vague' and 'obscure', but nothing like as 'vague' and 'obscure' as the prosecuting Judge Advocate's opening speech which occupied half a page in the minutes of the trial but swelled to eighteen pages in his closing speech. The closing speech was a farrago of legal errors, according to Brougham. 'Everything is twisted for the purpose of obtaining a conviction; and, which is the most monstrous thing of all, when the prisoner can no longer reply, new facts are detailed, new dates specified, and new persons introduced which were

[14] Parliamentary Papers 1824, Vol. 23.

never mentioned, or even hinted at, on any of the twenty-seven preceding days of the trial.'[15]

There are two accounts of Smith's trial; one is the official account printed in the Parliamentary Papers,[16] and the report written by William Arrindell, Smith's Counsel and published in London by the London Missionary Society.[17] The latter is the more complete as it includes comments of witnesses which were rejected by order of the Court and deleted from the official report. It also includes the passages of Scripture which in the Court's view were inflammatory when used by Smith, and an Appendix of letters, Mrs Smith's affidavit, and a copy of the petition presented to the House of Commons on 13 April 1824.

II

The Court opened on Monday, 13 October 1823, in the Colony House. It was Smith versus Demerara and, judging by the amount of space given to the trial and the attendant correspondence in the local papers, Smith was already a condemned man.

From his attic prison Smith was brought into the Court looking frail and plainly in the grip of a tubercular decline. He was a lonely man and his very loneliness is a mark of his trial and condemnation. Smith was meek and even mild and any civil judge would have wondered how such a subdued personality could possibly have been guilty of the charges brought against him. Even as late as 11 April 1824, when Smith had been dead and buried for two months, the *New Times* of London was still discussing the charges and wondering how Smith got the death sentence. According to the paper the vague charges could be sorted out into some sort of definiteness in this way:

[15] *Hansard*, 1 June 1824.
[16] Parliamentary Papers, 1824, based on the manuscript notes of the trial made by Mr Justice Wray sitting as an ordinary member of the court (Colonial Office Papers 1824:53).
[17] Council for World Mission Archives, with appendix of letters, etc., 1824.

1 That Smith had long intended to stir up rebellion in the Colony and had induced slaves to rebel against the lawful authority of their masters.

2 That he conspired with the slave leader Quamina and aided and assisted him when the rebellion was in progress.

3 That he gave no notice to the Government of the intended rebellion.

But was this enough to convict Smith of conspiracy and rebellion? Was it enough to convict him of 'misprison of treason' for which a capital sentence might be exacted? Could Smith be stigmatized as a traitor? Feelings were running high in Georgetown, particularly among the older members of the Colony who had been brought up under Dutch law which recognized the death sentence for withholding information when the safety of the state was imperilled.

If Smith could be lawfully condemned and lawfully 'hanged by the neck until dead', the Colony would have achieved a triumph over all that Smith symbolized. They would deliver a powerful body blow at the movement for improving the lot of slaves and all the ameliorating schemes of the English government. It was not just Smith who was up for judgement but the whole slavery emancipation movement itself. Hang Smith and you would once again re-assert the rights and privileges of slave ownership and show the world how to deal with rebellious blacks, and the soft-minded whites who sided with them.

So ran the talk of Georgetown as John Smith stood in the dock at Colony House for the long twenty-eight days of his trial. Length was important to the prosecution in order to impress the world with the Smith case and the detailed evidence was piled up in order to display the Court's care and attention. Smith, in the eyes of the Governor and Colony, was already guilty but the Court had got to prove what he was guilty of and without any doubts.

Much was made in Court of Smith's *Journal*, the little exercise book of diary pages which Smith kept from day to day. He was no Pepys or Parson Woodforde, but no one reading his *Journal* could be in any doubt that his mind and spirit were against slavery. He was easily depressed at its sights and sounds and especially when the Negroes were prevented by their masters from attending his chapel. Two entries for 25 and 26 December 1819 are typical of his diary style:

Saturday 25. This was certainly the most gloomy Xmas Day that I have known since I have been from England. The weather was remarkably fine, but the gloom was of a moral kind. Not a negro from any other estate than this came to the chapel. However, these people attended well. Several came from other places after Service to enquire why they were forbidden to attend the worship of God. I preached from Matt. 12.

Lord's Day, Dec. 26. I felt my mind much distressed all this day that the people were prevented coming to the House of God. The Lord gave me much liberty in prayer for them; nor did he forsake me in preaching the word, from Heb. 11, 24–26. Mr Kelly etc. were here. The conduct of Dr McT. is unaccountable; it is of mischievous tendency; for as well as being injurious to the negroes in a moral point of view, it is injurious in a political respect, by making them suppose their masters have combined to deprive them of their dearest privilege.

'Dr. McT.' as Smith calls him, was Michael McTurk, the local government officer for the Le Resouvenir area, an active opponent of any moves for slave freedom and a captain in the Militia. To see Smith on trial gave him much personal satisfaction.

Eighteen passages from Smith's *Journal* read to the Court proved precisely nothing except his own personal view that slavery was bad and ought to be abolished. Only one instance of exact advice contrary to government policy could be produced. It concerned the Governor's order of 16 May 1832, making it plain that slaves still had to get permission of their masters to leave the estate on Sundays to attend divine worship.

III

The first day of the trial was a formality which ended in Smith being given permission to seek legal aid. This must have been pre-arranged so that William Arrindell, a Georgetown lawyer, took up the case and steered Smith through the legal shallows and quicksands with remarkable skill. The routine of the trial was that the speeches of accusation and defence were supplemented by cross-examination of witnesses—chiefly those associated with Smith in the work of his church. The cross-examiners were the Judge Advocate and his assistants; and Smith himself through William Arrindell, his counsel.[18]

The three days' interrogation of the slave Bristol of Chateau Margo is typical of the proceedings as they were slanted to produce answers against Smith. The Judge Advocate cross-examines Bristol:

Was it also read to you why Moses went to deliver the children of Israel?—Yes, because they were slaves under Pharoah.
Did he read Exodus to you?—Yes.
Did he read Joshua to you?—Yes.
Do you recollect any particular chapter from Exodus?—No.
Do you recollect the purport of any chapter?—No.
Do you recollect anything from Joshua?—Joshua was the person who led the children of Israel after Moses was dead.
Was there any service performed in Bethel chapel besides on Sundays?—Once in a week besides Sunday.
On what day is that?—Thursday.
Is there no other night service but on Thursday?—Only on Thursday.
Did you ever see any whites at the morning service on a Sunday? —No.
Were they prevented?—No.

[18] In the printed account it looks as if Smith conducted his own defence, but evidently it was a legal custom of the period for a witness to be described as 'cross-examined' by the prisoner, though in reality it was the defence counsel speaking on behalf of the prisoner.

Were the doors shut during morning service?—No, the doors and windows were open.

Did you ever hear the Prisoner at prayer-meeting, or otherwise, say any thing about the treatment of the slaves?—Yes, sometimes when the people come to complain, and when they are hindered from coming to the chapel, and some of them get licked, then he tells them, well I cannot help that, but it is not right for your master to lick you and prevent you from coming to chapel.

Does the Prisoner listen to the complaints when the negroes come to him?—Only when they come to complain of what I have just now spoken of.

Did he never advise you or others what to do in case you had any complaint?—Yes, he said if there was any such thing, we must go to the fiscal or the governor, sometimes when the people ran away or so.

Any thing else?—That if the people run away they must not let them catch them again.

Do you remember when the governor's proclamation was read to the head negroes of the estates concerning going to church?—Yes. Did you hear the Prisoner speak about that proclamation?—Yes, he said that there was an order come out that all the people were allowed to come to chapel, that each owner was to give them a pass, and the overseer to come with them, and when they had done at the chapel, the overseer was to go back with them, and take them home; so far I heard.

The italicized questions were the ones that according to Bristol's later recollections the prosecution put into the report, for 'they wrote down more than the witnesses said, so anxious were they to catch every thing against Mr. Smith. I never said Mr. Smith told the negroes when they ran away not to let their masters catch them again.'[19]

Much was made of Jackey Reed's letter to the prosecution, regarding it as firm proof that Smith knew the rising was about to begin. Delivered to Smith by Jackey Dochfour, it read like a declaration of war ('the time is determined on for seven o'clock

[19] Proceedings of the Trial of J. Smith (Council for World Mission Archives); see also Wallbridge, E. A., *Martyr of Demerara*, p. 110.

to-night') from the high command controlled by Quamina and Jack Gladstone. As we have already seen, Smith played down the letter's flamboyant tone, but still it was a main piece of written evidence before the Court and was paraded with a flourish by the Judge Advocate during the evidence of Jackey's master, Lieutenant-Colonel Reed:

What are you?—A resident of this colony.
Where do you reside?—At Dochfour east coast.
Is there a negro of that estate called Jackey?—There is.
Do you remember the 18th of August last past?—I do.
Did you see Jackey on that night?—I saw Jackey on the night of the 18th of August.
Did he give you any paper?—He did.
Is this the paper which he handed you?—It is the paper.
Are you aide-de-camp to his excellency the commander-in-chief and Governor?—I am.
Did you wait on the Prisoner?—I did.
When?—On the Thursday or Friday of the first week's sitting of the court martial.
For what purpose?—To ask him for the letter which had been written and sent on Monday of the insurrection by Jackey Read to the Prisoner, which letter enclosed a letter from Jack Gladstone to Jackey Reed.

This visit of Colonel Reed to Smith in his room in the Colony House is an illustration of the vulnerable position Smith was in when unrecorded conversations were produced as evidence in Court. Reed appears to have reproached Smith with 'preaching very improper doctrine to the negroes', and with using the position of managers and overseers to illustrate his sermons, and so 'abusing' them. In his defence Smith dubbed this accusation as an instance of the 'aptness of negroes to misunderstand all that is said to them'. Reed finally admitted that the 'prisoner wished to impress upon my mind that if the negroes acted rebelliously, they must have misunderstood his doctrine'.[20]

The web of gossip and hearsay spun itself round Smith as the

[20] Proceedings of the Trial of J. Smith, pp. 49–50.

trial dragged on. All the petty talk of plantation life seemed to centre on the pale, shrunken figure in the dock, as one by one members of his congregation agreed to shreds of twisted evidence put into their mouths by the prosecution. The preliminary weeks of conditioning the slaves beneath the terror of the noose and the lash had done its work.

How much money was Smith making out of their church-going? How many Bibles, Psalm books and Catechisms did he sell? What about the supply of yams and chickens as presents? The issue of money passing into Smith's hands from his slave congregation was pressed so hard that Smith was forced to object that he was not on trial for 'fraudulent pretences', an intervention that was rejected from the official record of the trial.

IV

When it came to the evidence of W. S. Austin, Vicar of St George's Church, the Court moved on to firmer ground. Austin described his change of view regarding Smith and the insurrection and defended the right of a Christian minister to have personal intercourse with his parishioners. 'Were a minister to deny access,' he said, 'to those humble parts of his congregation, whose ignorance required them to be instructed, he would most effectually, except under a miracle, thwart the object of his public discourses. The spiritual wants and feelings of the humbler parts of my congregation can only be ascertained by personal application and intercourse, and I deem that one of the most important of my ministerial duties.'[21]

Austin was part of the Colonial establishment. His income and that of his church came from the Colonial Government, and every word of his in court that appeared favourable to Smith was a mark against him and his future prospects. He

[21] Ibid., p. 109.

sustained a lengthy duel with the Judge Advocate on Smith's relations to Negroes:

You say that the negroes complained to you that their religious duties were interfered with; was such a complaint ever made to you by any negro of your congregation?—Never; the complaints I mentioned were in reference to Mr Smith's chapel.

Do you refer to their language, when you say their complaints were uttered in an extraordinary style?—I do; their language and manner. One of their expressions used was, there was an attempt made to set down their religion, and that they would sooner die than give it up.

Did you see two negroes, Sandy and Telemachus, apparently engaged as leaders in this revolt?—I did see Sandy and Telemachus, and I think, from some expressions which escaped them, and from their manners, that they were possessing considerable influence, or actual leaders. Intelligence I have, since their convictions, received, convinces me that they were.

Was Sandy the man who said, in your presence, that they would not take life?— Sandy may have said that, but I heard the very expressions from several. I rather think Telemachus is the man upon whom I can charge it most positively.

Did any of these negroes ever insinuate that their misfortunes were occasioned by the Prisoner's influence on them, or the doctrines he taught them?—I have been sitting for some time as a member of the committee of inquiry; the idea occurs to me that circumstances have been detailed there against the Prisoner; but never to myself individually, in my ministerial capacity.

Austin neatly dodged giving his imprimatur to the revolutionary text, Luke 19:41, 42, by describing it as 'one of the most beautiful texts of Scripture' and being sorry he had not preached from it himself!

Smith also protested at the misuse of his private journal, and the attempt to incriminate him because of certain entries about the 'grumbling of negroes' and the working of slaves on Sundays. But when he brought out his Bible and began to read evidence from the Scriptures on the obligation to keep the Sabbath holy and free from work, the President quickly shut him up, on the

---

grounds that the members of the Court could read the Scriptures at home. Unnecessary labour on Sundays was a sin to Smith, as it was to Moses, Jeremiah, Nehemiah, Ezekiel, Isaiah and Christ himself, all of whom Smith was eager to quote in support of his Sabbatarian claims. He knew that the lazy managers who wanted their late Sunday breakfast of freshly caught fish could easily shatter attendances at chapel. They could refuse to give a chapel-going pass until the fish was caught, grilled and served, and in any case passes were anathema to Smith as an infringement of personal liberty. A Negro could be flogged for going to chapel without a pass, and a manager could be fined 600 guilders under Colony laws for making him work on Sunday, but only the first penalty was ever inflicted.[22]

Smith and his Bible were up against a formidable combination of antique laws and customs, all loaded in favour of slave owning as property to be managed according to the owners' whims and fancies. Smith calmly let the slave society speak for itself. A more ambitious preacher and talkative prisoner would have roused all the latent ferocity of his opponents and even won them some sympathy. Smith's tactics were simple, even gentle. He let the slave society tell its own story and expose its own iniquities, and endured the consequences in his own frail body and patient spirit.

'Neither myself nor my doctrines were the cause of the revolt,' he pleaded in his final defence. Only upon the confused and contradictory slave evidence could the prosecution make any case against him, while Smith was able to point to the powerful evidence of the fiery Colonel Leahy, as well as the Rev. W. S. Austin, that they had never heard his name mentioned among the slaves in revolt.[23]

[22] Ibid., pp. 74–5.
[23] Ibid.

V

Then followed a day-long speech by the Assistant Judge (also called John Smith!) which once more surveyed the whole case and built up a subtle decimation of the prisoner's character as a secret planner of revolt. On the grounds that a 'missionary of the Gospel has sown, amongst his negro flock, the seeds of dissatisfaction, with interest to rouse them to rebellion', the prosecutor declared :

The crime presupposes great secrecy and great caution, for the criminal is placed in a situation of extreme delicacy, where one false step, one precipitate movement, either on his own part or on the part of the negroes, may at once ruin all his projects. He must hold out one character to the world, and another to the negroes. He must endeavour to conceal even from them the end he has in view, else their rashness may betray him; and he must thus strive to poison the minds of his victims, without their being themselves aware of the hand which administers the potion.

He admitted that the prosecution had had a difficult task in getting legal proof of their charges, particularly from members of Smith's congregation 'which has been for years under the thralldom of the criminal himself'. In examining a 'leading feature in the prisoner's system' of reading key Bible passages to his congregation, the prosecution alleged that the deliverance of the Israelites was his favourite reading, and that he was careful to read it at the early morning service when no whites would be present. 'Not only their masters were held up to slaves as opposing religion, the highest authorities in the Colony were represented as pursuing the same course; and it is impossible not to observe with how much contempt the prisoner has generally treated the commands of government. The effects of such an example would not fail to be felt.'[24]

'Go which way we will,' exclaimed the prosecutor, 'we are brought up at last with Bethel chapel. The only bond of con-

[24] Ibid.

nexion to be traced amongst the leaders of this rebellion is their being attendants of Bethel chapel. There must have been some pre-disposing cause, operating on the members of Bethel chapel —something operating on them which did not operate on the negroes on the other coast.'[25]

It was Smith's purity of doctrine, systematic teaching and skilful management of the good and obedient slaves which brought on the revolt. If the slaves were dissatisfied, then he had no right to trade on their dissatisfaction. If they were 'oppressed, persecuted human beings obliged to eat raw yellow plantains and being constantly flogged' why were they able to make presents to him and raise money to repair the chapel?

The prosecution alleged inconsistency in the defence, and finally attacked Smith's own integrity by asking why it was that obedient slaves, after listening to Smith's preaching, rose in open rebellion against their masters? 'What must we think of the doctrines which have been preached to them?'[26]

Covered in legalized obliquy, and loaded with emotive words such as 'criminal', 'revolt', 'rebellion', 'guilt', 'traitor', 'rebel', Smith listened to the prosecutor's closing words to the Court as he 'threw himself on your candour'. Smith's plea was a solemn declaration of 'my innocence'.

At the twenty-eighth day of the trial, on 24 November, the Court assembled and found Smith guilty of promoting discontent among slaves, but not guilty of directly inciting to open revolt 'for want of sufficient proof in support thereof'.

He was guilty of aiding and abetting the Negro Quamina and of communicating with him at the beginning of the revolt, but not guilty of further assisting. On the third charge he was found guilty of not making known to the authorities that a revolt was intended and fourthly of not making any attempt to seize and detain the insurgent Quamina.

It was enough. Smith had imperilled the peace of 'our Sovereign Lord the King, his crown and dignity and in defiance

25 Ibid.
26 Ibid.

of the natural law'. Whether it was treason or merely 'misprison of treason' was of no consequence. The Colonists' Court had pinned their victim to the scaffold 'to be hanged by the neck until dead', without any hint of an appeal and with the full consent of the Governor.

There followed a most extraordinary loss of nerve. The Court had secured its victim but as the solemn words of the death sentence were read it revealed its inner misgivings about the whole proceedings and especially about the legality of the sentence just passed. Smith was recommended to mercy. 'Is it possible,' asked Brougham in the House of Commons, 'to draw any other inference from this marvellous recommendation than that they distrusted the sentence to which it was attached?' Brougham saw the Court in full flight with guilty consciences for having 'dared to take this innocent man's life'. Nothing in the trial 'is so astounding as this recommendation to mercy coming from persons who affected to believe him guilty of such enormous crimes'.[27]

Smith left the Court a condemned man but also a victorious one. By his simplicity and meekness he had exposed the slave system and had faced the worst that an all-powerful Colonists' court could inflict on an accused person. He had eight weeks to live, and during those eight weeks the emancipation of slaves in British possessions became inevitable.

'The calumniated minister' (Brougham said) 'had so far humanized his poor flock—his dangerous preaching had so enlightened them—the lessons of himself and his hated brethren had sunk so deep in their minds, that, by the testimony of the clergyman, and even of the overseers, the maxims of the Gospels of peace were upon their lips in the midst of rebellion, and restrained their hands when no other force was present to resist them.'[28]

[27] *Hansard,* 1 June 1824.
[28] Ibid.

APPENDIX TO CHAPTER SIX

John Smith's Trial—The Evidence

On the twenty-fifth day (14 November 1823) of the twenty-eight days' trial Smith, through his counsel, closed his defence and proceeded to give some comments on the evidence produced against him :

It is evident, from the evidence, that I have always acted with greatest uprightness and integrity; that I have gone further, and conducted myself with prudence and caution, from the time of my arrival in the colony to the revolt; nay, Hamilton proves, that even in the very midst of the attack on his house, I hastened to his assistance, and used all the means I possessed in his favour; that I exhorted the negroes to be quiet—it was all I could do.

All the negroes, both for the prosecution and defence, who were questioned on this point agree, that I always taught them to be obedient to their masters, and to submit themselves to all in authority over them; not an individual exception is there to this train of evidence. My journal, read from page to page, will not disclose any single passage emanating from bad feeling towards any individual. The vices and follies of some may have therein been reprobated; but, even the reprobation of those persons was confined to myself; I did not commit, in many instances, even their names to paper.

The certificates, from the various proprietors and managers of the states on the west coast, abundantly shew, that, even in the performance of the rite of baptism, I was peculiarly cautious, with respect to the characters I admitted into my congregation. George Donaldson states, that 'as the pass given was not sufficient, he would give another'. Nicholas Van Cooten says, that 'finding I was wishful of some testimony of the negro's character, he therefore recommended'. But had the negroes been excited to disobedience by me, would I have required testimonials of character, before I bestowed upon them, what they considered a valuable acquisition. These facts certainly carry with them conviction that I never did and never could intend, either directly or indirectly, any the least injury to their owners, to the government, or to themselves. With this conviction, I will enter upon the first part of the second and the third charge.

It has been attempted, and, in fact, the whole drift of the prosecution of the charges, and of the questions of the Prosecutor, was to shew that the religious negroes were the most refractory and rebellious. What do the certificates of baptism say? That only they were recommended by their owners, managers, or overseers, who behaved well, who were well-disposed, and who were thought worthy of reward. Do not all these proofs, from even interested parties, clearly demonstrate, that the effect of religious instruction was beneficial? Independently of this, the witnesses, H. Van Cooten himself a proprietor of one and attorney of another, large estate, and John Stewart, unwilling as he was to answer my questions, have sworn, that the religious negroes were the most obedient in general. Every planter, every master can tell how very untractable and unruly is a dissatisfied negro. He will not be obedient. The series of written evidence proves that those negroes who were allowed to attend the chapel, conducted themselves in a dutiful manner.

It is a bold assertion, but not more bold than true, that there is not a single negro-witness upon any material point, either in support of the second and third and fourth charges, or in support of the defence, who is not either contradicted by himself, or by some other witness. In some part of his evidence, Bristol contradicts himself; he is also contradicted by Emanuel, Seaton, Peter, Shute, Mary Chisholm, and Charlotte. Emanuel (or Manuel) is contradicted by Bristol, Seaton, Mr Stewart, Mr Elliot, Mary Chisholm, and Bill. Seaton is contradicted by Bristol, Peter, Shute and Charlotte. Peter is contradicted by Bristol, Seaton and Shute. Shute is contradicted by Bristol, Seaton and Peter. Charlotte is contradicted by Peter and Shute—Ankey is contradicted by Elizabeth; and Elizabeth is contradicted by Ankey, Dora and Mr Hamilton.

Which of these witnesses is the one to be believed? They are all alike, they are all at variance with each other; and whether one is to be selected in preference to the rest, or all are to be discredited, is a matter to be determined solely by the Court. I think I have shewn, that it will require at least some determination to discover the one worthy of any credit. They cannot all be believed, no two of them can be believed together; three of them have certainly made use of the word drive, it was not the word that Quamina used to me, and how the negroes have got hold of it is obvious to everyone. They have drivers, who drive them to their work, the word is more familiar to them than any other word, they have used it among themselves, and now they hesitate not to assert, under oath, that Quamina used it to me; but let me remark, that, under the same oath, they have asserted other parts of the conversation, which unfortunately for themselves, are contradicted by each other, in every way possible.

The evidence, in fact, is such as to render it impossible for any one to say, that, from it alone, the real truth can be ascertained. That negroes are not verbally accurate in general, is not only well known and proverbial, but has been proved by H. Van Cooten, a resident among them for fifty years. He swears he would not intrust even a common message to the memory of any of them, for ten to one if they would carry it correctly, though some might do so. I need not tell this Court, we do not want suppositions, but positive assertions in a case of this nature; negroes may speak to facts, but in their notions of time, and in verbal accuracy, they are miserably deficient; and, even had there been no positive evidence on this point, it would have been apparent, from the evidence of the negroes, both of the prosecution and defence.

I must observe, that it is impossible to come to a conclusion upon any one of the charges, without taking the whole evidence into consideration. If this be done, it is manifest, that neither myself nor my doctrines were the cause of the revolt; that my name, as connected with the conduct of the revolted negroes, was not even mentioned by any of them. Mr Austin declares, he went up amongst them prejudiced against me, yet he in his examination says, 'I must add, that in no one instance, among my numerous inquiries did it appear that Mr Smith had been in any degree instrumental to the insurrection'. Lieutenant-Colonel Leahy, who was in command of the whole coast, was amidst the negroes on every occasion, and had every circumstance worthy of notice conveyed to him, says, 'I don't recollect hearing the Prisoner's name mentioned till I came to town'. Take then Hamilton's evidence, that of Stewart, Elliot and Davies; and what will not their testimony weigh against a number of ignorant negroes, under the influence of their masters; under the fear of punishment for their conduct; and, therefore, glad to throw blame upon any one, rather than allow it to remain with themselves, as it really does; contradicting themselves, contradicting each other; and no two of whom agree in any material point.

On the twenty-seventh day (19 November) the Assistant Judge Advocate, John L. Smith, made his comments on the evidence as prosecutor:

The congregation, he said, which the Prisoner collected around him, consisted of the unbaptised, of the christians, as those were more particularly termed who had been only baptised; the members of the chapel, who were admitted to the sacrament of the Lord's supper; and the deacons; besides these, there were, on the different estates, classes, each under its own teacher, who was nominated, or at least sanctioned, by the Prisoner, as is proved by Romeo and Bristol.

In his public sermons he sometimes tells them to be obedient to their masters; but, when it is reduced to any one specific circumstance, he does not hesitate to hold forth the very opposite doctrine. But the Prisoner, in the present case, was not contented with merely telling Jacky to disregard his master's order, but he actually sent him, in defiance of these words, to a meeting of the negroes at plantation Orange Nassau.

On the head of keeping the Sabbath, the Prisoner prohibited the negroes from working on that day in their own grounds, going to market, or even washing their clothes, under pain of incurring the vengeance of their Creator. Whatever he may urge on this point, I believe there is no one who looks at the constitution of society in this colony, but will, without hesitation, admit that there exist no means so well calculated to render the negroes dissatisfied as this very one, to deprive them of their Sunday, the day which they have to themselves; and you find, gentlemen, by the positive testimony of Manuel and Bristol, uncontradicted by any one witness, that this measure did produce the effect to be expected. That the negroes began to murmur, and require another day for themselves, and that this was one of the great causes of that dissatisfaction, which at length drove them to open rebellion.

The time which he chose for reading the Bible is also to be observed; it was not at noon-service, where whites might sometimes be found—no, it was at the morning-service, when whites never came. He rests much on the circumstance that the doors were open, and that whites might have come; but the very licence under which he preached at all, bound him not to close the chapel doors; besides, the shutting of them might awaken suspicions, and experience had fully assured him, that there was no likelihood of a white coming to the service. But not only their masters were held up to the slaves as opposing religion, the highest authorities in the colony were represented as pursuing the same course; and it is impossible not to observe with how much contempt the Prisoner has generally treated the commands of the government. The effects of such an example would not fail to be felt.

Thus far, however, I may go, and observe that there is great inconsistency in the defence of the Prisoner; in one part he describes the negroes as the most oppressed and persecuted of human beings, who have not, in the cotton crop, fifteen minutes in the whole day to eat their food; none to cook it, and are, in fact, obliged to eat raw yellow plantains; and all the time they are constantly flogged. At the same time, gentlemen, it has been proved that these negroes, aye, even the field negroes, can afford to make presents to him, raise money to pay the expenses; nay, more—the repairs of the chapel—to buy books at an advance of 66 per cent on the original cost in England, and to contribute to the Missionary Society, to further the propagation of the gospel in other countries. How these miserable beings contrive this, passes my comprehension. In much the same style the Prisoner accuses the planters of opposing religion, and preventing the negroes attending chapel. Yet the Prisoner hands over to you a host of passes from these planters to their negroes, to have them baptized; and he tells you, and proves it, that though his chapel had been enlarged, yet it could not contain all the congregation, and that numbers were obliged to remain outside every Sunday.

The conduct of the Prisoner through the whole appears, from beginning to end, one consistent system, one uniform plan; and, therefore, in judging of intention, it may be taken altogether; but the parts which I have thus far detailed, seem to form the groundwork of the first charge; and I beg leave, ere I proceed to the next charge, to bring before you, in one vein, the various points which I conceive already proved.

These are, that the Prisoner possessed great influence over his congregation; that he was ever ready to receive and listen to the complaints of the negroes; and frequently, in these cases, advised them to disobey and disregard their masters.

That he taught them to consider their masters hostile to religion, and exposed by their conduct to the indignation of the Almighty.

Which interference with the master, and which representation of him, inevitably tended to destroy all their confidence in him, and to degrade him in their eyes.

That, further, the negroes were taught by the Prisoner to look on themselves as persecuted for religion; that there existed great irritation and dissatisfaction amongst them, and that they murmured at not having a day to themselves.

That, though the Prisoner well knew that their minds were thus irritated, and though he was well aware that they would pervert, and take, as applicable to themselves, any passage which could at all be brought to bear on their situation as slaves, he yet read to them the history of the deliverance of the Israelites from Egypt, and of the wars of the Jews, and explained it to them in words most exactly fitting their own condition, that he led them, by example and precept, to treat lightly the orders of government.

The extracts above are taken from the report of the Smith trial published by the London Missionary Society in 1824. The account, presumably written by William Arrindell, Smith's counsel, is from the copy in Sion College Library, London.

CHAPTER SEVEN

'Your useless but devoted Servant'

John Smith was now a condemned man.

From the ordeal of the court martial he was taken to face the ordeal of the colony jail, marked by the stigma of the death sentence which Murray approved, although he softened its harshness by sending the recommendation for mercy to London.

This seasoning of justice was not the colonists' idea of dealing with Smith. 'Hanged by the neck until dead' was what they wanted for the man who had so subtly defied them in organizing the insurrection. Thwarted from seeing his living body hanging from the gallows they hung his effigy there as a substitute. Blood they must have and this was the nearest they could get to it.[1]

To them Smith was guilty of a mortal affront to the slavery system in which they moved and had their being. He had modestly and meekly questioned the foundations of their way of life, which not only gave them a livelihood but also provided one for many honourable men of property beyond the seas.

Smith had not only affronted a caste in Demerara but had acted as a secret agent for those misguided politicians and philanthropists in Britain whose ultimate aim was the complete abolition of the slave society. In condemning Smith they were condemning Wilberforce and Co., an exercise they thoroughly enjoyed.

To cap their celebrations, as Christmas 1823 drew near, Governor Murray exhorted slave managers and overseers, by proclamation on 16 December, to distribute 'Christmas cheer' to their slaves. 'Let there be no work on Christmas Day', he said,

---

[1] Wallbridge, E. A., *Martyr of Demerara*, p. 132.

and even on the day following there should be indulgence and rest up to midnight.

This saturnalia had its limits. Not on 'any pretence or consideration whatsoever' was it to apply to the East Coast of the Colony, from Georgetown to Mahaica. There in the heart of the insurrection country the unrelieved gloom of primitive justice was to proceed as the hangings and floggings were meted out to the convicted rebels.[2]

During his Christmas in the colony jail the condemned man contemplated the wreck of his seven years' mission work. He had little to show for his preaching, and signed himself in his last letter to London 'Your useless but devoted Servant'. In the damp, dreary isolation of the jail, exhausted by the weeks of an unjust court martial, Smith was understandably depressed. But need he have been?

Although Bethel Chapel appeared to be the headquarters of the revolt, twelve of the ringleaders came from estates where no one had been baptised by Smith. A careful analysis made in May 1824 showed that out of 2,000 people baptized by Smith not more than five or six were executed and only one out of 200 communicants. Twelve of the ringleaders lived on estates where no one had been baptized by Smith.[3]

Among the ringleaders known personally to Smith were Quamina, shot in the bush, Jack Gladstone of Success, his son, reprieved after turning 'King's evidence', Telemachus of Bachelor's Adventure, a communicant who was executed; Paris of Good Hope, executed after clearing Smith of his previous accusations. Baptized members of the church also executed included Daniel and Philip of Foulis, Billy of Ann's Grove, and Paul of Friendship.[4]

None of the ringleaders appears to have come from Smith's own plantation of Le Resouvenir, which may have been evidence of their contentment, or of their obedience to listen to Smith on

[2] *The Colonist*, 18 December 1823.
[3] Wallbridge, op. cit., p. 135.
[4] Ibid., pp. 201ff.

5—SM • •

the night of 18 August, as he tried to clamp down on the rising.

Thinking back to the events of August, Smith justified himself to London. 'I am bold to affirm that I never gave utterance to anything that could make the slaves dissatisfied with their condition.'[5] Struggling to work in the enclosed humidity of his damp room, Smith surveyed the evidence of the court martial and came to the simple conclusion that with no firm evidence of the origin of the revolt the colonists fastened on him as the 'main cause'. He thought it significant that none of the negroes who gave evidence against him was punished.

I

Jane Smith too joined in the epistles to London, giving her account of 'the temporary ruin of the missionary cause in this colony', and apologizing for her husband's imprisonment as the reason for his not writing. 'I myself have been but a few days liberated from a rigorous imprisonment of thirteen weeks with him.'[6]

Jane believed that the real cause of the slaves' revolt was 'political', a thrust for freedom, but that the colonists had substituted 'religion' as the original impetus:

Many of the planters, I think I may say the Colonists generally, apprehended that the religious instruction of the slaves was incompatible with their condition in life, and that as soon as they became a little enlightened, they would revolt; and many of them believed, or pretended to believe, that the real object of Missionary instruction was, by instilling into their minds principles of insubordination, to make them revolt; and, though the proximate and chief cause of the revolt was evidently of a political nature, yet that was overlooked, and religion substituted in its stead.

[5] Smith to Burder, 12 December 1823 (Council for World Mission Archives).

[6] Jane Smith to Burder, 4 December 1823 (Council for World Mission Archives).

'Your useless but devoted Servant'

To His Excellency
Major General John Murry
Leint. Governor
&. &. &.

Sir

In consequence of the decease of my late husband I have determined upon leaving the Colony as soon as the formalities required by law can be observed. I have therefore respectfully to solicit your Excellency to order the restoration to me of all Books, and Papers belonging to my Deceased husband which were required and taken possession of by the persons who arrested him — particularly the Journal which contained many matters of a private nature which I am sure Mr Smith would not have made public, and which on that account I should like to be preserved in the privacy intended.

There is also a great part of the Money taken away from Mr Smiths house on his being arrested still unpaid, of this I am in great need — your Excellency will therefore I trust be pleased to order the immediate payment to me of the Balance.

I have the Honor to be
Your Excellencys
Most obedient
humble Servant
Jane Smith

Jane Smith to Governor Murray after her husband's death

She was also more inclined to believe that 'our Chapel' was the centre of the revolt storm than the evidence warrants:

It is alleged that most of the people that attended our chapel were engaged in it. That many of them were implicated is, I am sorry to say, too true. From the nature of things it was hardly possible it should have been otherwise. It is further said, that the plot was formed by men that attended the chapel, and that one of our deacons was a ringleader.

She really saw through the colonists' strategy in their 'go for Smith' plans:

Having us both in close confinement, the legal authorities and the planters set to work with all their might to rake together something in the shape of evidence to condemn us. They examined scores, I believe, I might say hundreds, of persons; and after near seven weeks' labour, in this way, they preferred against Mr S. those serious charges which they supported by the evidence you see.

Prejudice and ill-will won the verdict against her husband:

How the Court Martial could justify a conviction on such evidence, must, I think, be a wonder to every unprejudiced person. But the verdict of a Court Martial is decided by the majority of its members; several of the members of this Court were much prejudiced against Mr S., and two of them at least could not refrain from showing their ill-will towards him on the trial. Here, at present, almost all are prejudiced against Mr Smith, from the highest to the lowest.

She then pays a graceful, womanly tribute to W. S. Austin, the Vicar of St George's and Chaplain to the garrison, for his belief in her husband's innocence. 'In spite of all opposition, from the commencement of this persecution he stood up as a warm friend for Mr Smith.' Finally she pleads to the Missionary Society to use 'every exertion in behalf of Mr Smith, whose greatest crime was his devotedness in the object of his mission'.

Jane Smith's letter was one of the first communications to reach London after the Court's verdict, and to alert the London

Missionary Society that Demerara was producing a dramatic
crop of problems. Fortunately two very able officers were then
in executive charge of the Society's affairs, George Burder,
Secretary until 1827, and William Allers Hankey, Treasurer
until 1832. Between them they had immediate access to the
Anti-Slavery Movement, then making its new momentous effort
towards emancipation, and to the Colonial Office. Whitehall
received its official account of the court martial in mid-January
1824 and William Arrindell's parallel report to the London
Missionary Society arrived soon afterwards. Burder, with
remarkable celerity, had the Arrindell report edited, printed and
published by the early spring so that when Brougham rose to
call the attention of the House of Commons to the case of
'missionary Smith' on 1 June 1824 the name of John Smith
was as well known as that of David Livingstone thirty years later.
Parliamentary Papers called for ran to 230 closely printed
foolscap pages, a prodigious number for one man's case.

II

Early in January 1824 Smith gathered his failing energies to write
to London for the last time to make plain his belief that what
had really happened was an attack on religion by the planters.
He quoted from the *Guiana Chronicle* for 11 February 1822 to
illustrate the deep 'rancour and fury' of the planters:

We have had occasion repeatedly to express our opinion of the
sectarian propagandists, who send forth their missionaries out of
a pretended zeal for the salvation of souls. They, the missionaries,
to be sure, are too wise and cunning to make direct attacks from
the pulpit on public men and measures; but in respect of their
wild jargon, their capricious interpretations of the Bible, and the
doctrines they inculcate, although in themselves they are to be
despised and slighted, yet, in point of the pernicious tendency they
may have upon the minds of their hearers, we do think no caution
can be too great, no vigilance too strict. Instances are not wanting

of their imposture in this part of the world; their manner of raising revenue in support of their church, is not unknown; neither is the way in which the contributions are sacrilegiously squandered. That fact alone ought to weigh against all their solemn professions of being actuated solely by a pure love of godliness and apostolic zeal in the cause of Christianity.[7]

As a 'useless burden' the dying man wondered whether his superiors in London were apprehensive about his real intentions. Had he abandoned his original calling? Had he 'diverted his mind' from his missionary obedience? Was he really innocent, or was there some truth in the planters' charges? A 'kind and sympathizing letter' from London, dated 19 November 1823, assured him of the esteem and confidence in which he was held, and that he was innocent of the crimes laid to his charge.

But Smith, still sensitive, feared that those who originally sent him to Demerara were shaken in their confidence. His emaciated frame and the airless, humid condition of his confinement all contributed to his depression. The 'Lord's hand is heavy upon me', he wrote, and 'he has brought me to the borders of the grave'.

Smith might well have been more depressed had he known that in Britain alongside the rising tide of sympathy and concern for him which made 'Smith the Missionary' a *cause celebre,* there rose an organized opposition to all that his 'case' stood for. At the heart of the movement was John Gladstone, M.P.

Gladstone regarded the Demerara rising as an example of the work of that 'well meaning but mistaken man Mr Wilberforce' and all those 'more intemperate, credulous, designing or interested individuals who have placed themselves in his train'.[8] Gladstone saw the 'unfortunate slaves' as 'deluded, deceived and misled' and scoffed at the idea that 'free slaves' would work more willingly. His information was that 'manumitted negroes are idle, indolent, slothful and too often become profligate, though

---

[7] Smith to Burder, 12 January 1824 (Council for World Mission Archives).
[8] *Liverpool Courier,* 13 October 1823.

they possessed good characters whilst they remained slaves'. As for Smith, Gladstone was shocked that he 'is reported to have administered the Sacrament to the ringleaders the evening before, and recommended that they should be sparing in the effusion of blood'.[9]

Gladstone was stirred to action by the news from Demerara and took the lead in forming the British Guiana Association to protect the interests of the planters, and to build up opposition to the emancipators and their programmes of slave amelioration. Gladstone's propaganda skill also made sure that the lines of communication with the Government through Canning, the Foreign Secretary, Huskisson, of the Board of Trade, and Bathurst, the Colonial Secretary, were kept open. Huskisson declared his belief that Smith had been 'an accessory before the fact to the rising', and that he had established an 'organised system of influence through his deacons and regulations'. This kind of missionary, said Huskisson, must be replaced by more docile clergy of the Church of England, who, while enjoying the benefits of the establishment, were also under its direct control.

Not content with 'dealing with Smith' privately in official quarters, Gladstone engaged in a public warfare of words with his old friend James Cropper, the Liverpool Quaker philanthropist who attacked slavery in a letter in the *Liverpool Mercury* of 31 October 1823. Gladstone replied in the *Liverpool Courier* and the two former friends continued arguing for eighteen letters, Cropper exposing the iniquities of the planter system and Gladstone defending the planters in justice and in law. He compared the happy lot of slaves in the West Indies with the miseries of the peasants in India who were more exploited, abused and deprived of prospects of improvement. No one read the letters more eagerly and carefully than a fourteen-year-old boy at Eton—William Ewart Gladstone.

[9] Ibid., 4 December 1823.

III

What puzzled John Gladstone more than anything was the fact that his own Demerara plantation of Success, whose old chimney is now a historic Guyana landmark, had been at the heart of the slave rising. How was it that his own slaves, well treated and seldom punished, rose in revolt and provided its ringleaders? Either Frederick Cort, his attorney, had deceived him with his mild, humane reports, or the derided London Missionary Society and its agent, Smith, had engineered the rising.

He chose to believe the latter and threatened the Society with legal action over the false reports it was spreading through Britain. Gladstone was warned by the Society's Treasurer, William Allers Hankey, that the information in the possession of the Society showed that Cort had deceived him, and that in any public discussion the Society 'will feel it their duty not to decline the task'. Gladstone recognized the danger signal, and much to the relief of his wife and daughter, withdrew from public altercation about 'Missionary Smith'.

But Gladstone did not withdraw from Demerara! In fact the rising, and its ill effect on the reputation of the anti-slavery movement in the eyes of the government, persuaded him to thrust deeper than ever into plantation owning. To Gladstone it looked as if the abolition of slavery had been postponed, perhaps for another generation, so there was still time for more money to be made out of the fruitful soil of Demerara. His plantation Success had truly earned its name: out of a capital investment of £80,000 he got an income of £10,000 a year!

While Smith languished his last weeks in the Georgetown jail Gladstone was busy negotiating for the purchase of the Fileen estate of Vreendenhoop, across the river from Georgetown, which he eventually brought off to the tune of another £80,000 and considered it a bargain.

Gladstone persuaded himself that abolition of slavery was still a long way off, and that to possess more plantations and more slaves would give him greater authority on West Indian affairs in London and especially in the House of Commons. So he studied new methods of sugar production and got them going in Demerara to produce better and cheaper sugar, and sent his son Robertson to stay for three months in Demerara. He came home with the comforting report that although Cort, their attorney, was quite as bad as the missionary society said, yet slavery was still idyllic and 'will remain so, if allowed to live undisturbed by the meddling and ill disposed'—a sentiment that his brother, young William Ewart, just going up to Oxford, heartily supported. The Gladstones by then owned over a thousand slaves.

IV

John Smith was dying. He could no longer sit up to write or to read. His shrunken frame, wracked with coughing, crouched in the corner of the damp room, while Jane Smith, aided by the faithful Mrs Elliott, watched over him. Austin, the clergyman, Chapman, the doctor, and Padmore, the kind-hearted jailer, completed the little group that saw Smith's life gradually fade away.

On 24 January 1824 the jail surgeon informed the military secretary that Smith had 'extreme debility'. Next day the secretary authorized the surgeon to take whatever steps necessary for 'Smith's re-establishment' that the Governor would approve. A week later the surgeon replied that short of removing Smith to a better climate there was nothing he could do, and on 5 February he reported 'Mr. Smith appears to be at the hour of death'. He died the next day, 6 February, at half-past one in the morning.

At 8.30 a.m. the Governor was informed of Smith's death, which set in train a series of macabre events.

As a condemned felon Smith's burial was the responsibility of the Colony's law officers and at the inquest at 5 p.m. His Honour the First Fiscal displayed all the pomposity of colonial bumble-dom regarding Mrs Smith's rights. Asked about the cause of her husband's death, Jane Smith boldly claimed that 'false accusations, persecution and imprisonment' had hastened his 'pulmonary consumption', a reply that infuriated the Fiscal. Mrs Elliott was even bolder and charged the Fiscal with conducting an illegal inquiry. Threatened with the power of the law to make her answer his questions, the unquenchable Mrs Elliott still defied him, and the Fiscal wisely withdrew.

At eight the same evening the two women, keeping guard over Smith's body, were visited by the prison constable with the news that the Governor had ordered the burial for 4 a.m. next morning, and that no one would be allowed to follow the corpse to the grave. Sensing the possibility of some public demonstration, as the news of Smith's death spread round Georgetown, Governor Murray avoided a daylight burial time and chose the early morning hour and banned a funeral party. He reckoned once again without the resolution of the two women, so well expressed by Jane Smith : 'General Murray shall not prevent my following my husband to the grave, and I will go in spite of all he can do.' His Excellency capitulated with the compromise that the women met the corpse at the grave without actually following it.

With lanthorn lit at half-past three o'clock, as the early dawn came up over Georgetown, and escorted, appropriately, by a 'free black man', the two women stood by the grave dug in the yard of the jail, or more probably on land where St Philip's Church now stands. Mr Austin read the burial service, committed the body, the grave was re-filled and the earth stamped in.

John Smith was buried at last and no mark or monument to this day has ever been erected to show where he lies. The attempt of a couple of negro members of his church to rail in the burial plot was stopped by the First Fiscal, the bricks scattered and the railing torn down.

When he heard the news of Smith's death the planter John Gladstone wrote to William Huskisson of the Board of Trade : 'I was not sorry to hear of Smith's death, as his release would have been followed by much cavil and discussion.' It was a sentiment deplored by the Gladstone ladies but welcomed by 'young Willy', who had much admiration for his father's political judgement: the elder Gladstone reckoned without 'Missionary Smith' being more powerful dead than alive.

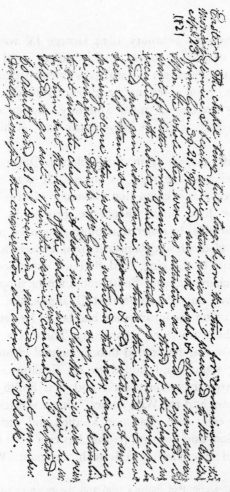

Easter Monday April 23 1821
A typical entry in his *Journal* by John Smith, a full chapel

CHAPTER EIGHT

John Smith marches on

At Windsor on 14 February 1824 George IV was signing his daily ration of official papers. In his spidery hand he scrawled the royal signature across the stiff parchment papers, transforming them into royal commands and official directives. The king enjoyed this exercise of royal authority, particularly when it affected life and death decisions dependent on his own royal prerogative.

One of the papers from the Colonial Office was in this category and was regarded as urgent. It was the Colonial Secretary's recommendation that Governor Murray's request for clemency for John Smith should be granted by the king as quickly as possible, in order that Smith might be released from his sentence of death and banished from Demerara.[1]

In a minute to the king Lord Bathurst explained that in his opinion the charges against Smith could not be supported on the evidence. Even on the charge that Quamina, the rebel leader, visited Smith after the insurrection had begun he 'remained there for a very short time, and went away. There is no evidence of the prisoner having harboured him or assisted in his escape.'

The king signed and added to his signature : 'I approve entirely of your recommendation and that Smith be expelled from Demerara and the West Indies.'[2] But it was too late. Smith was already eight days dead and he died and was buried as a convicted felon, and no royal pardon has ever been forthcoming. No Colonial Secretary faced with rampant West Indian

[1] The official account of Smith's trial and the recommendation to mercy were sent to London on 2 December 1823.
[2] Colonial Office Papers III/42.

interests, both in the House of Commons and in Demerara, would have recommended it, and posterity was conveniently relieved of its responsibility by Smith's speedy death by natural causes.

The *New Times* of London thundered against the Governor for having brought Smith before a court martial, and wondered what pretence there could be for trying a minister of the Gospel after this manner. 'We have been struck with horror at the idea of bringing into jeopardy of his life a man whose conduct does appear to us, on an impartial review of the whole evidence, to have been not simply blameless but most meritorious, most exemplary.'[3]

Like John Brown of Virginia, John Smith of Demerara went marching on.

In the profligate, absolutist society of England in the reign of George IV, the Smith story shone in modest splendour as a triumph of humanitarianism and Christianity. Smith was no wordy pundit and no extrovert prophet, and modestly wrote himself down as 'useless' but 'devoted'. But after him 'slavery' was never the same. He had exposed its decayed foundations, and revealed the horrors of regarding human beings as profitable property.

In his brilliant critique of the slavery emancipation movement Eric Williams accuses Wilberforce and his 'saintly' colleagues of being familiar with 'what went on in the hold of a slave ship but ignored what went on at the bottom of a mine shaft' in England. They were not radical reformers but conservative capitalists, and while their humanitarian motives were admirable they did not originally contemplate the complete emancipation of slaves. It needed the *trauma* of the Smith case to convert them to complete emancipation. Even then, Williams says (quoting Buxton) there was to be 'nothing rash, nothing rapid, nothing abrupt, nothing bearing any feature of violence'. In fact the emancipators looked to the slave owners themselves to bring about abolition, hoping

[3] 17 April 1824.

that slavery itself would gradually decay, die away and be forgotten.[4]

But John Smith had almost unwittingly uncovered the roots of slavery and shown them to be far deeper than even Wilberforce and his colleagues sometimes believed, and that the slaves themselves, as well as their owners, were concerned about their condition and their future.

Economic forces plus religious and humanitarian ones finally brought about emancipation, says Eric Williams. The outworn interests of the West Indies 'whose bankruptcy smells to heaven' could be still powerfully obstructive but they finally succumbed to the newer capitalism drawing its resources from the East and from the new industrial wealth in Britain.

But if it is allowed that 'missionary Smith' is a turning point in the abolition and emancipation movement, then the deeply laid forces of humanitarian Christianity cannot as a whole be ignored. It is to the credit of Georgian England that, unreformed though it was, low in morals and riddled with graft, yet it nursed this great movement that appealed to the innate sense of religion in the English character.

I

John Smith, though dead, became the emotional symbol of the emancipation cause in its final stages, and as his story spread through the country it stirred men to action. On 13 April 1824 the pioneer petition of the London Missionary Society was presented to the House of Commons and this led to a nation-wide flow of petitions, culminating in the mighty avalanche of 1833.

According to *The Times* of 24 May 1824 Lord Stanley led the way at the bar of the House with a Lancashire petition in company with Lord Francis Osborn from Royston; Sir Thomas Acland, Barnstaple; Mr Stuart Worsley, Desborough. On 28

[4] Williams, E., *Capitalism and Slavery* (1944), p. 182.

May Sir William Guise of Stroud captained a further team—
Mr Jervoise, Hampshire; Mr C. Smith, St Albans; Lord
Uxbridge, Anglesey; Mr N. C. Smith, Norwich; Mr Buxton,
Camberwell; Mr Newman, Exeter; Lord George Cavendish,
Ingatestone; Lord John Russell, Hitchin and Baldock; Lord
Belgrave, Chester; Mr Rumbold, Great Yarmouth. Altogether
there were over 200 petitions presented to the Commons in
eleven days, harvesting thousands of signatures collected by eager
enthusiasts. The petitions rehearsed in sonorous language the
facts of Smith's trial, the iniquities of slavery and prayed the
'honourable House to institute such inquiries, or direct, or adopt
such measures as may best tend to obtain a revision or rescind-
ment of the sentence passed on Mr. Smith'.[5] It was all a
powerful propaganda prelude to the memorable 'Smith debate'
of June 1824 when, as we have seen, Henry Brougham magnificently excoriated Smith's accusers and saluted the humble
missionary as worthy of the name of martyr.[6]

Macaulay crowned this victory with his own eloquence at a
meeting of the Anti-Slavery Society on 25 July 1824 when he
described Smith's trial as 'more insensible to justice than any
Star Chamber'. He tore to pieces the argument that Smith got
a fairer trial by court martial than he would have done by a
jury of planters. If this was so it was an admission that invited
the strongest condemnation, and revealed the hollowness of the
proceedings.

'Poor Smith the missionary died in prison at Demerara',
lamented Wilberforce; 'the day of reckoning will come.' Smith's
death had dealt a blow to British slavery from which it never
recovered: he had delivered its death warrant.

[5] London Missionary Society's Petition, 13 April 1824 (Council for
World Mission Archives).
[6] See Plumb, J. H., The *First Four Georges* (1966), p. 174. Oddly enough
Roger Fulford in his *George IV* makes no reference to the abolition movement. He refers once to Wilberforce's dining magnificently with the Prince
Regent at Brighton in 1815 and Wilberforce's comment 'how ill suited
to the baptismal engagement to resist the pomps and vanities of this
wicked world'.

II

There was no such victorious salute for Smith in Demerara itself. Within a couple of weeks of his death the colonists convened a public meeting to insist that the 'missionary system' Smith represented should be eradicated in the colony, and the press was in full cry in warning the colonists that a continuation of 'education' and 'religion' would spell the end of the happy relations between owners and their slaves.

'If we expect', said *The Colonist*, 'to create a community of reading, moral, church-going slaves we are woefully mistaken. It is not the smallest matter of surprise that a negro slave, who has taught that all men are equal in a religious point of view, should wish the same principle to prevail in politics!'[7]

Smith's preaching had gone home. The Bible was seen to be not just a book of personal religious piety but a manifesto of liberty which demanded to be taken seriously in the relations of man to man as well as between man and God.

If this kind of preaching, said the *Guiana Chronicle*, was not to be tolerated then the 'missionary system' must go, for the 'independent missions' are a threat 'to the feeling of mutual dependence and attachment which united master and slave and which, as it was the firmest basis of our security, was the fairest and most promising source of substantial benefit and improvement to the slave'.[8]

Smith dead appeared to be a peril to the colonial system even more than Smith alive, according to the pro-slavery London paper *John Bull*:

Advantage is taken of Smith's death to effect a purpose which could not have been accomplished had he lived. That purpose is to intimidate the Governors and Governments of other colonies from the discharge of their duties in perilous cases and times, to prostrate them at the feet of every agitator who may well call himself a Missionary, and by the terror of a thousand petitions, and the

[7] 18 February 1824.   [8] 27 February 1824.

consequent proceedings in Parliament, to give an ascendancy to a class of persons who, whether intentionally or not, are, we are perfectly convinced, most dangerous to the very existence of our system.[9]

By the time *John Bull* had spoken its mind, Governor Murray had been recalled, and from his lodgings at 42 Craven Street, Charing Cross, was preparing to answer the fourteen questions put to him by Lord Bathurst on the 'Smith case'—an inquisition (see Chapters 4 and 5) that revealed the official unease about Murray's conduct.[10] Ironically enough Murray received his letters of recall on 7 February 1824, the day after Smith's death. Alive or dead there was no escaping Smith! But he did not rob Murray of his Companionship of the Bath in 1824!

Within the shadow of Smith's death and posthumous fame the government took heart to press forward with its 'mitigation' or 'amelioration' plans in the colonies under its immediate control.

There were still over a million human beings in slavery under British rule, an uncomfortable thought for humane men like Canning and Bathurst and one which they were regularly reminded about on the floor of the House of Commons by Fowell Buxton and his fellow anti-slavery men.

III

The more Buxton and Wilberforce meditated on the significance of the Smith case, the more they realized that 'amelioration' was no final answer. Smith meant abolition and emancipation. But as old tried campaigners they were ready to accept 'amelioration' as another stage on the road to their final goal. 'We now have an acknowledgement on the part of Government', said Wilberforce in the House of Commons,' that the grievances of

[9] 13 June 1824.
[10] Colonial Office Papers. III/44.

which we complain do exist, and that a remedy ought to be applied.'[11]

Canning's orders of 1823 (see Chapter 4) were reinforced by the new order of 10 March 1824 which commanded and cajoled the twelve colonies concerned to see that slaves were not worked on Sundays, were not whipped without the presence of a witness and with not more than twenty-five lashes in one day. Female flogging was to be abolished, marriage was to be encouraged and families not dispersed by sale. Slaves could purchase their freedom at a price to be settled by arbitration, the testimony of slaves accepted in a court of law, and religious instruction provided. This was as far as the powerful West Indian interests would allow Whitehall to go in its 'amelioration' programme, comforted by the thought that the practical application of these orders still fell within the delaying tactics of any prevaricating governor such as Murray of Demerara had proved to be.

By 1826 it had to be admitted by both government and abolitionists that very little had been done as a result of the 1824 orders and Canning himself reported his 'disgust' at the slowness of change. In the 1826 Commons debate Brougham once again moved a resolution 'touching the condition of slaves' and elicited the information that out of twelve colonies ordered to 'ameliorate' their condition eight had provided religious instruction, eight had begun to regulate flogging, seven were prepared to admit slave evidence, five had abolished whipping of females and five were prepared to arrange marriages.

It was a slow march to freedom, if indeed freedom was the aim of the orders and directives from Whitehall which sped across the seas to the colonial legislatures. Speaking on their behalf Wilmot Horton reminded the House of Commons that every step recommended was fatal to the interests of slave proprietors. It all tended to 'depreciate if not destroy their property',[12] and was an invitation to suicide.

[11] *Hansard*, 15 May 1823.
[12] *Hansard*, 19 May 1826.

The alert Brougham was quick to respond to this rejoinder and to hoist the warning signal of parliamentary authority. The trial of John Smith had taught him to recognize colonial bumble-dom when he saw it and he warned planters and legislatures of the dangers of flouting the will of Parliament. The House had an opportunity of letting it be known to the West Indian legislatures, who had disregarded the wishes of Parliament, that the time had at length arrived when, if they did not do their duty, Parliament was determined to do it for them.[13]

IV

During the seven years following Smith's death Britain was a land of reformation in which the claims of Catholic Emancipation (1829), Electoral Reform (1832) and Slavery Emancipation (1833) were kept regularly before Parliament and people through the zealous country-wide propaganda of their devoted adherents. A combination of well-timed pressure, through petitions, public resolutions and parliamentary tactics achieved these reform victories—a powerful mixture of human appeal, political wisdom and spiritual warfare.

Within the anti-slavery movement Smith's pathetic story, com-bined with that of his wife, for whom a public subscription was raised on her return to Britain, naturally made its appeal to women, and was one of the primary causes of women's interest in the later stages of the slavery crusade. Up to then it had been a masculine venture but the revelations associated with 'Mission-ary Smith' drew in the powerful concern of women. They found a living movement to support and in 'the petition' an instrument to wield with enthusiasm.

In 1828 the 'women of Leicester' pioneered with an appeal to 'the hearts and consciences of British women', followed by the 'Ladies of Lyme Regis' who in 1833 presented a petition to the House of Lords condemning slavery as 'an insult to the feelings

[13] Ibid.

of every female on earth'. In the same year a demonstration of 1,800 Glasgow ladies was convinced that 'the fervour of their zeal must soon dissolve the fetters of the slave', and the Females of Britain produced 350,000 signatures for their petition.

Petitions to the House of Commons—most of them boosted through the hard work of local women linked in hundreds of small societies—flowed in full flood as the slavery debate of 1833 reached its climax. In February and March it was fifty a day, at the end of April 200, rising to 300 and then 500 on 14 May when Lord Stanley presented the Abolition Bill. To warn the House of Lords of the state of public opinion petitions to them swelled to 1,200 on 14 May and again on 17 May.[14]

Neither Whigs nor Tories could claim all the political credit for these movements of reform and emancipation, and particularly in the case of slavery the parties were well mixed. Even families such as the Gladstones, were divided, with young Mr William, as late as 1833, still proclaiming his faith in the planters and their slave property, while his mother bemoaned the family association. But slave emancipation had the united support of the Irish party in the House of Commons, for their leader, Daniel O'Connell, claimed that from Cape Clear to Giant's Causeway Ireland was abolitionist in heart and action.

During these years successive governments gradually came to the conclusion that in effecting slave reforms the method of 'authoritative amelioration' had run its course. Lectures to the distant colonies from Downing Street on how planters were to deal with slaves, and how legislatures were to enforce regulations, had little effect. The Tory Lord Goderich, then at the Colonial Office, admitted this failure in his 1831 dispatch when he wrote 'advice has been but little listened to in any of the colonies and in some of the most important and considerable has been more than once rejected'. The government, he said, 'had

---

[14] Hurwitz, E. F., *Politics and the Public Conscience,* pp. 62, 90, 92. In the autumn of 1830 petitions ran to 2,600, with 2,200 of them from Nonconformists.

ceased to entertain hopes that their admonitions will ever prove efficacious.[15]

The fate of Smith had exposed the obduracy of the planters and their entrenched determination to resist forms of amelioration suggested from Britain. Goderich's dispatch recognized that 'advice' had now to give way to 'orders' and 'hopes' to 'compulsion'. The hand of Britain had to be revealed with strength if planters were to be jolted out of their bastions and slaves given a new measure of freedom.

The dispatch talked warily about 'substantial relief to the West Indian interests', while in fact it was the herald of the British Government's intention to buy out the planters to the tune, eventually, of £20 million. The dispatch was, once more, eloquent about 'improving the condition of slaves', but in fact the government was coming to the conclusion, dogged by the shadow of Smith, that the colonies concerned could no longer exist 'half slave' and 'half free'. It had to be Abolition and Emancipation, with all the risks involved.

It was the Whig Lord Stanley who eventually in 1833 put these conclusions into a parliamentary bill, with its first clause 'that immediate and effective measures be taken for the entire abolition of slavery throughout the colonies' being passed in the House of Commons without a division.[16]

Clause four put teeth into the bill. It suggested provision of compensation to slave owners amounting to a loan of £15 million. Slaves were said to be worth at least £40 a head, which could put the compensation money as high as £30 million. Young Mr Gladstone reckoned his father's slaves were worth over £50 a head.[17] Eventually the compromise of £20 million, as an outright payment to slave owners, was reached and Wilberforce made his historic comment 'Thank God I should

[15] Parliamentary Papers, 1831–2. Henry Brougham caustically remarked that the action of slave owners in relation to amelioration was 'so slow as to be imperceptible to all human eyes save their own'.
[16] *Hansard*, 30 May 1833.
[17] See Chapter 2.

have lived to witness a day in which England is willing to give twenty million sterling for the abolition of slavery'.[18]

Remembering Smith and the Demerara rising many owners prophesied that freedom would mean chaos on the plantations and confusion in their relations with their former slaves. They insisted on an elaborate apprenticeship system to help them through the change-over but their worst fears of lawlessness proved ill-founded.

It so happened that the news of freedom was given to Demerara by a governor whose name, appropriately, was Smyth —Sir James Carmichael Smyth. After explaining the Act and proclaiming Emancipation Day to be on 1 August 1834, he said:

I trust you will all return to your work quietly, happily, and cheer-fully, and that in your prayers you will not fail to return your humble and sincere thanks to the Almighty God for having thus opened the door and prepared to lead you from the house of bondage. The wisest and ablest men never anticipated that such a great and blessed change could have been effected in your favour, but at a remote period and even then accompanied with blood-shed.... Prove yourselves worthy of the blessing of freedom and show yourselves loyal and obedient subjects of that truly paternal government to which you owe so much.[19]

Sir James Smyth had been on Wellington's staff at Waterloo but he spoke with the accents of John Smith, humble missionary of Demerara, and one-time London biscuit baker.

V

The slave emancipation movement in England began as an aristocratic venture in politics and philanthropy but developed

[18] Wilberforce, R. I. and S., *The Life of William Wilberforce* (1838), Vol. 5, p. 370. The final amount disbursed in settlement of all claims was £18,669,401.
[19] *Anti-Slavery Reporter*, 26 December 1833.

into a popular movement, including all ranks of society. John Smith, in this sense, was a representative man who deserves a place among the exalted names of Wilberforce, Buxton, Brougham, Stephen, Clarkson and the rest of the noble company of emancipators.

A decade elapsed between John Smith's death in 1824 and Emancipation Day in August 1834 but in those ten years his story was an ever-present, pungent reminder of the immense human price that had been paid to abolish slavery. The plantation owners got their millions and, according to the economic ethics of the day, were entitled to their prize.

But Smith from his forgotten grave spoke for the other high price, in countless human beings, that had been paid for reformation and freedom. He represented the miseries of bondage, the subservience of black to white, the hangings and the floggings which for two centuries had helped to sustain Britain's sugar slave empire. His own death had been part of the price paid for emancipation—a fact that adds abiding honour to his name and story.[20]

But there were other and even more profound and permanent results arising from abolition, especially in Britain's West Indian colonies. The notion was born that men were equal, and that the old demarcations of 'master' and 'slave' had been abolished. No one could go back to the old order; a new world of brotherhood was emerging.

The outpouring of the anti-slave protest in Britain also created a new sense of responsibility towards 'colonial peoples'. It could be dubbed 'paternalism', and at its worst 'imperialism', but it also produced a wealth of unselfish service which paved the way for twentieth-century 'independence'.

Abolition awoke too in Britain a 'conscience' about Africa, and the unpayable debt that the white man owed to the black in that continent. The horrors of slavery and their effect on Africa and its peoples could never be wiped out by Acts of Parliament.

[20] Mrs Jane Smith died at Rye, Sussex, on 10 February 1828, aged thirty-four.

They demanded a continuous and disinterested concern. The abolition of slavery was the achievement of economic forces combined with a long-drawn parliamentary campaign, aided by a popular propaganda movement of religious fervour. That achievement was secured through the devotion of many great men, but at the heart of the battle were countless little men, such as John Smith.

Across the Atlantic the American abolition movement gathered much of its inspiration from the British achievement. The Quakers of Pennsylvania, the intellectuals of New England, and the mid-west men who ran the 'underground railroad' for escaping southern slaves all looked to the British emancipation leaders for guidance and encouragement. In 1833 William Lloyd Garrison, the American abolitionist, went to England to see the dying Wilberforce, and his later visits confirmed him in his 'frontal attack' on the institution of slavery.

The situation in the two countries was significantly different. To abolish slavery in their overseas colonies did not threaten the British way of life, but a similar action in America menaced the very basis of society that America was creating. The slave sugar kingdoms of the West Indies produced wealth for a favoured few in Britain, but the slave kingdoms of cotton were vital to the existence of the American South.

The anti-slavery speeches of the pacifist William Lloyd Garrison, and the open warfare of John Brown, were essentially American in character and not within the British pattern of achieving emancipation. John Smith could never have been John Brown, and the old warrior of Harper's Ferry would have scorned the 'meek and humble' Smith, as he did many of the New England intellectuals. The two men lived at the strategic watersheds of the anti-slavery movement in their respective countries, and they challenged the presence and power of slavery in all their grim inhuman corruption, and they were both involved in insurrections that heralded its ultimate collapse.

Both were convicted of conspiracy and treason, and died for their convictions. Awaiting his execution on 2 December 1859

John Brown wrote to his children that he was content 'to die for God's eternal truth on the scaffold as in any other way'. Awaiting his slow death in January 1824 John Smith scribbled on the back of a money bill drawn, ironically, to pay for his own illegal trial, the Biblical reference '2 Corinthians, IV, 8 9', which reads : 'We are troubled on every side, yet not distressed; we are perplexed, but not in despair; persecuted, but not forsaken, cast down, but not destroyed.'

When William Lloyd Garrison heard of John Brown's escapade he remarked : 'John Brown has merely told us what time of day it is. It is high noon, thank God.'[21] The same might have been said of John Smith.

Postscript

In the old Stabroek Market in Georgetown today stands an ancient sugar grinder turning the handle of his antique machine squeezing out the last drop of sweetness from his little stock of canes. Not far away, along the water front of the Demerara River, is the massive apparatus of a modern sugar mill which delivers the sugar straight from the cane to the ship's hold for the world's markets.

Sugar is still king of Guyana. In the century and a half since the insurrection sugar has retained its pre-eminence. It is still basic to the economy of the Co-operative Republic of Guyana. The soil of the plantation belt still yields its rich crop of sugar cane, much of which is still harvested by hand in a manner that the owners and managers of John Smith's time would easily recognize.

As you drive up the east coastal road towards the Berbice River the long swathes of the sugar cane stretch endlessly at right angles from the road. The dirt tracks then plunge 'into the bush' to the villages and hamlets with their chapels and schools.

21 Nye, R. B., *William Lloyd Garrison* (1955).

Guyana is nearly ninety per cent literate, an achievement that no emancipation prophet of Smith's day would have thought possible.

The tall chimney of Plantation Success rises by the roadside, a signal to ships approaching the mouth of the Demerara River, and a noble relic of the insurrection. Not far from it is a handsome white mosque, a sign of the presence and power of Islam in modern Guyana.

On the plantation acres of Le Resouvenir at Beterverwagting is Bethel Chapel, a lineal descendant of the one built by the pious planter H. H. Post in 1807 for John Wray to preach in. Post died in 1809 and his tomb is a place of pilgrimage. Bethel Chapel contains memorials to John Smith and Quamina of Success.

John Smith's other memorial in Georgetown stands within the churchyard of the Smith Memorial Church on the Brickdam. It is a simple bust and looks out to the spacious street not far from where he spent his last hours.

But the living memorial to Smith and the insurrection is Guyana itself. Its trend today may be towards 'communism' and its most lively co-operators the Soviet Union and the Chinese People's Republic, but its first taste of freedom came when people of 'African descent' dared to assert that they were brothers to all men, and proceeded to put the truth into action and accept the consequences. John Smith and his colleagues were only aiders and abettors in that process.

Sources

Council for World Mission (formerly the London Missionary Society). Archives are at the London School of African and Oriental Studies in West Indies boxes—Guiana, Berbice and West Indies and British Guiana and the special John Smith boxes. I have used E. C. Cheveley's manuscript *Journal* for the first time. The L.S.O.A. issues a descriptive booklet of the archives (1973).

Public Record Office. Colonial Office Papers, C.O.111, pp. 42–53.

United Society for the Propagation of the Gospel. The U.S.P.G. began its work in British Guiana after Smith's time but it has papers relating to W. S. Austin who befriended Smith.

Cambridge University Library. Parliamentary Papers and *Hansard*, and printed books.

National Archives, Georgetown, Guyana for Letter Books.

L.M.S. Report on J. Smith, 1824, Sion College Library.

PRINTED BOOKS CONSULTED

Anstey, Robert T., Capitalism and Slavery, a critique, *Economic History Review*, Second Series XXI No. 2 (1968)

Bennett, G. W., *History of Guiana* (1866)

Brown, K. F., *Fathers of the Victorian Age; the Age of Wilberforce* (1961)

Burn, W. L., *Emancipation and Apprenticeship in the British West Indies* (1937)

Buxton, Sir T. F., *Memoirs* (1848)

Chamberlin, D., *Smith of Demerara* (1924)

Checkland, S. G., *The Gladstones* (1971)

Clarkson, T., *History of the Abolition of the African Slave-trade* (1839)

Coupland, R., *Wilberforce: A Narrative* (1923)

Coupland, R., *The British Anti-Slavery Movement* (1933)

Dunn, R. S., *Sugar and Slaves* (1973)

Edwards, B., *The History of the British Colonies in the West Indies* (3 vols. 1793–1801)

Furneaux, R., *William Wilberforce* (1974)

Griggs, E. L., *Thomas Clarkson, the Friend of Slaves* (1936)

Hawes, F., *Henry Brougham* (1957)

Hennell, M., *John Venn and the Clapham Sect* (1958)

Howse, E. M., *Saints in Politics, the Clapham Sect and the Growth of Freedom* (1952)

Hurwitz, E. F., *Politics and the Public Conscience* (1973)

Klingberg, F. J., *The Anti-Slavery Movement in England* (1926)

Lascelles, E. C. F., *Granville Sharp and the Freedom of Slaves in England* (1928)

Lovett, R., *History of the London Missionary Society*, 2 vols (1899)

M'Donnell, A., *Considerations on Negro Slavery* (1824)

Mathieson, W. L., *British Slavery and its Abolition* (1926)

Morley, J., *The Life of William Ewart Gladstone*, 3 vols (1903)

New, C. W., *The Life of Henry Brougham to 1830* (1961)

Nye, R. B., *William Lloyd Garrison* (1955)

Plumb, J. H. *The First Four Georges* (1966)

Pope-Hennessy, J., *Sins of the Fathers* (1967)

Ragatz, L. J., *Fall of the Planter Class in the British Caribbean, 1763–1833* (1928)

——, *A Guide for the Study of British Caribbean History, 1763–1834, including the Abolition and Emancipation Movements* (1932)

Rain, T., *Life of John Wray* (1892)

Rice, C. D., *The Rise and Fall of Black Slavery* (1975)

Stephen, G., *Anti-Slavery Recollections* (1854)

Stephen, J., *The Slavery of the British West India Colonies Delineated*, 2 vols (1824, 1830)

——, *England Enslaved by her own Slave Colonies* (1826)

Wallbridge, E. A., *Martyr of Demerara* (1848)

Ward, W. E. F., *The Royal Navy and the Slavers* (1969)

Sources

Wilberforce, R. I. and S., *The Life of William Wilberforce* (1838)

Wilberforce, W., *Appeal to the Religion, Justice and Humanity of the Inhabitants of the British Empire on Behalf of the Negro Slaves in the West Indies* (1823)

Williams, E., *Capitalism and Slavery* (1944)

NEWSPAPERS AND PERIODICALS

This is an important source for comment and for a judgement of public opinion. The 'Smith case' from 1824–6 was a constant theme of feature articles and news commentary. In Britain *The New Times* and *John Bull* gave most attention, with *John Bull* as the bitterest opponent of the anti-slavery party. The *Anti-Slavery Monthly Reporter* (whose editor was Zachary Macaulay) was launched in 1825 on the wave of popular interest surrounding 'missionary Smith'. The *Annual Register* is a useful factual record for the years 1817–26.

INDEX